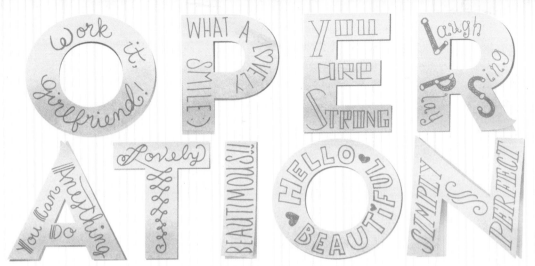

OPERATION

One Note at a Time

BEAUTIFUL

by Caitlin Boyle

Grosset & Dunlap

An Imprint of Penguin Group (USA) Inc.

Tired of hearing her own inner voice telling her she wasn't good enough, blogger Caitlin Boyle scribbled "YOU ARE BEAUTIFUL!" on a Post-it, stuck it on the mirror of a public bathroom, took a picture, and posted the photo on her blog. A movement—OperationBeautiful.com—was born. Caitlin has been featured on the *Today Show* and the Oprah Winfrey Network (OWN) and in magazines such as *Glamour*, *Fitness*, and *Self*. She was also chosen by Yahoo as one of the "Top 10 Inspiring Acts of 2010." Additionally, Caitlin runs Healthy Tipping Point, a food and fitness blog that encourages others to redefine true health and happiness. She is the author of *Operation Beautiful: Transforming the Way You See Yourself One Post-it Note at a Time* and *Healthy Tipping Point*.

To every girl who ever felt like she wasn't good enough: You're even more amazing than your wildest dreams. You're beautiful—just the way you are. This book is for you.

GROSSET & DUNLAP
Published by the Penguin Group
Penguin Group (USA) Inc., 375 Hudson Street, New York, New York 10014, USA
Penguin Group (Canada), 90 Eglinton Avenue East, Suite 700, Toronto, Ontario M4P 2Y3, Canada
(a division of Pearson Penguin Canada Inc.)
Penguin Books Ltd., 80 Strand, London WC2R 0RL, England
Penguin Group Ireland, 25 St. Stephen's Green, Dublin 2, Ireland
(a division of Penguin Books Ltd.)
Penguin Group (Australia), 250 Camberwell Road, Camberwell, Victoria 3124, Australia
(a division of Pearson Australia Group Pty. Ltd.)
Penguin Books India Pvt. Ltd., 11 Community Centre, Panchsheel Park, New Delhi—110 017, India
Penguin Group (NZ), 67 Apollo Drive, Rosedale, Auckland 0632, New Zealand
(a division of Pearson New Zealand Ltd.)
Penguin Books (South Africa) (Pty.) Ltd., 24 Sturdee Avenue, Rosebank, Johannesburg 2196, South Africa

Penguin Books Ltd., Registered Offices: 80 Strand, London WC2R 0RL, England

Copyright © 2012 by Caitlin Boyle. Published by Grosset & Dunlap, a division of Penguin Young Readers Group, 345 Hudson Street, New York, New York 10014. GROSSET & DUNLAP is a trademark of Penguin Group (USA) Inc. Manufactured in China.

Library of Congress Control Number: 2011040297

ISBN 978-0-448-45756-7

10 9 8 7 6 5 4 3 2 1

ALWAYS LEARNING

PEARSON

OPERATION BEAUTIFUL

One Note at a Time

Table of Contents

Introduction

Do you ever feel like you just aren't good enough?

For a long time, I worried *all the time* about being second-best. I wanted to be the smartest girl in my class, and I wanted to be popular. I wanted to own all the coolest clothes and gadgets. Most of all, I wanted to be as beautiful as the women I saw in magazines.

My middle school had a strict dress code. The biggest issue was the length of your shorts. If you were standing with your arms by your sides, your shorts had to be at least as long as your fingertips. Sometimes, though, I felt like that was still too short! I studied the backs of my legs in the mirror, worrying about how my thighs looked. When I sat down at my desk, I agonized over how my skin became all dimply—I later learned this was cellulite, a natural occurrence that happens to

> Most of all, I wanted to be as beautiful as the women I saw in magazines.

most women, regardless of your size. Eventually, I became so paranoid about my thighs that I stopped wearing shorts most of the time. I felt more comfortable with my legs covered up.

No one ever teased me about my thighs, so I can't say exactly how I developed this mental hang-up. I was teased about the size of my breasts, the pimples on my chin, and the color of my hair. (I had an unfortunate incident with a box of hair dye when I was twelve years old and walked the halls with orange-hued locks for at least a year!) The teasing hurt. But more than anything, it pained me to look at magazines. I couldn't help but compare—I didn't look anything like the gorgeous, perfect models.

I just wasn't pretty enough, I decided. And I probably wasn't smart or popular enough, either.

One night, I was talking to my

friend on the phone, whispering so my mom wouldn't hear me. "More than anything, I am afraid of being mediocre," I confessed. "Sometimes it's all I can think about!" (*Mediocre* means something is neither good nor bad; it's barely acceptable. To me, mediocre was the worst kind of ordinary.) When I finally said my secret out loud to someone else, it was like a lightbulb went off in my head.

It pained me to look at magazines.

I wouldn't raise my hand in class because I was afraid I would look stupid—even if I was pretty sure of the answer. Whenever I felt particularly plain and ugly, I would walk around with a frown on my face, my shoulders hunched around my ears, and my head down. This body language certainly didn't do any favors for my appearance, and it probably made me seem so unfriendly. In reality, I was just nervous that others were judging me and wouldn't like me. In a nutshell, I was fulfilling my own greatest fears—I was holding myself back with a lot of negative noise!

Word Up Negative Noise

Do you ever think something about yourself that you would never, ever say about a friend? That's negative noise. Negative noise is negative self-talk, which includes things you think to yourself and say out loud to other people. One example of negative noise is telling a friend, "I feel like a pig in this dress!" when she says she likes your outfit. Even if you don't really mean it, negative noise is harmful because it can add up and impact the way you see yourself. Negative noise can also come from other people; for example, bullying is a very serious form of negative noise.

My friend agreed. "It makes me so upset when you put yourself down," he told me in a sad voice. "Instead of being the best version of you, you waste a lot of energy trying to be someone else."

I was fulfilling my own greatest fears—I was holding myself back with a lot of negative noise!

Have you ever flown on a really small plane? You don't walk directly onto the plane; you have to walk outside and climb up the stairs that extend from the plane's door. It is always supernoisy outside, and you can barely hear anything besides the rumbling of other engines or the roaring wind. I like to think that all of my bad thoughts are really loud, useless noise. When my mind is filled with negative noise, I cannot really think of anything else—and I certainly cannot reach any of my goals.

After that fateful phone call, I decided to really *tune in* to my negative noise so I could learn how to *tune it out*. Whenever I felt my brain filling up with the roar of negative noise, I thought about what those negative thoughts were really trying to say. If I said or thought something bad about my body or personality, I asked myself why I thought those things. Sometimes I would write my thoughts in my journal. Over time I realized that I was often just nervous, sad, or upset about something else. So every time the negative noise crept back into my life, I replaced it with a positive thought. "You CAN ace this test; you studied so hard!" I'd think. "I love my legs—they let me run so far in cross-country!"

I like to think that all of my bad thoughts are really loud, useless noise.

It wasn't always easy to be so positive—life can get really confusing! If I slipped up and let the negative noise back in, I would just remind myself that I had the power to change my thoughts. My thoughts became my actions, and my actions became . . . well, my life! I couldn't control everything around me, but my thoughts were my life, however I wanted to experience it. It could either be negative or positive, and I wanted to choose the happier route.

And that is exactly what Operation Beautiful is all about—choosing the positive over the negative. To participate in Operation Beautiful, all you have to do is write an encouraging message on a sticky note and post it in a public place, like a bathroom or dressing room. When you write an Operation Beautiful note, the positive message has an impact not only on the lucky person who finds your note, but also on your own self-esteem.

I was twenty-five years old when I posted the first Operation Beautiful note. It was late at night, and I was stuck at night school at the community college. Recently a new form of negative noise had reared its ugly head—I didn't like my job anymore and decided I was going to go back to college to learn new skills. But the classes were *so* hard, especially when I had to work all day at my job. Without even realizing it, I had slipped back into my old negative noise habits!

I excused myself from class and went to the bathroom. Standing at the sink, I stared into my tired, sad eyes in the mirror. All these horrible thoughts went racing through my head: "You aren't smart enough for chemistry . . . how are you going to afford another round of college? . . . you're totally going to bomb this exam." I was about to burst into tears when I suddenly realized the negative noise had gotten hold of me! Inspired to change my thoughts, I rummaged through my purse and pulled out a sheet of paper, a pen, and a camera.

> Without even realizing it, I had slipped back into my old negative noise habits!

I scribbled the truest message in my heart—*You are beautiful!*—and stuck the note on the mirror. I smiled as I took a picture of my note.

The first Operation Beautiful note

Would someone struggling with negative noise walk into the bathroom after me? I hoped the note would make that girl realize that no matter what was happening in her life, she was a unique person who was worthy of love and respect. I wasn't just saying that whoever found my note was beautiful on the outside; what I really meant was that she had the inner beauty to tackle any challenge. Just as I had the power to change my thoughts and change my life, I wanted someone else to see that they could do it, too.

✴ Do It Now! ✴ Post an Operation Beautiful Note

Grab a packet of Post-it notes and a marker. Write down your favorite mantra. A mantra is a motivational phrase like "You can do it!" or "You're strong and talented!" Stick the note in a public place, like on a bathroom mirror or in a dressing room. If you write the operationbeautiful.com website at the bottom of the note, whoever finds it can go online with a parent's permission and learn more about the movement.

When I got home, I uploaded the photograph of my note to my computer and blogged about it. I wanted the whole world to feel as good as I did at that moment. I called my new mission Operation Beautiful and asked other people to participate, too. I wasn't sure anyone would actually follow my lead, but just a few hours later, the notes started to roll in. My e-mail exploded! I had notes from New York and San Francisco, from Chicago and Dallas. I got notes from ten-year-olds and moms, from college students and grandmas. Just three days later, I decided to launch the operationbeautiful.com site, and the movement truly took off.

The e-mails kept coming, and the stories became more and more amazing. Teenagers who were tired of bullying at their schools covered bathroom mirrors with hundreds of positive messages and reported that everyone seemed a bit nicer that day. Friends went to the mall and put an Operation Beautiful note in every dressing room. I began to receive notes in Spanish and Chinese and hear stories from teenagers in France and Brazil. People from all over the world had come together to stamp out negative noise—and it was all happening because of one little piece of paper.

And then—I started to hear from the people who *found* the notes. Amazingly, some people came across a note when they needed the positive message the most. Shut out by her former friends, a lonely girl discovered an Operation Beautiful note in her locker. It read, "Stand tall! You're an amazing person." A woman who had just filed for divorce from her husband found a note in the bathroom at the courthouse. A tired cashier noticed a positive message written on the back of a dollar bill. "I know it sounds strange, but Operation Beautiful saved my life," confessed one depressed teenager.

I wanted the whole world to feel as good as I did at that moment.

Every day, we make a million decisions—many of them simple and some of them very hard. Perhaps the most basic decision we all must face is whether to believe in ourselves and our own abilities. Operation Beautiful has helped me more fully understand that we are the creators of our own future. I hope this book helps you become a more confident, happy girl. This ability is already inside you—you just have to unlock it. And all that's required is a Post-it note and a pen.

Above everything else, remember this: You are beautiful. Together, let's count the ways.

Journal It: Your Favorite Motivational Mantras

Writing is a great way to learn more about yourself, sort through problems, and keep track of awesome memories. Throughout this book are prompts called "Journal It" with fill-in-the-blanks, questions, and scenarios for you to write about. So grab a notebook and a pencil—it's time to start your Operation Beautiful journal.

My favorite thing to write on an Operation Beautiful note is, "Life doesn't happen to you; make life happen for you."

What are your favorite motivational mantras? Create a list in your journal. You can even write a new, positive phrase at the top of each entry! There are tons of examples of mantras throughout this book. You can also write down positive song lyrics or lines from movies!

Madeline, Ohio

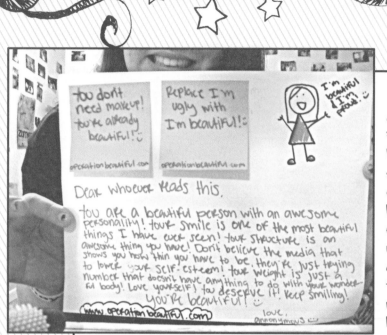

I'm thirteen years old, and I can honestly say that Operation Beautiful has changed the way I look at myself and others. Ever since I was six, I've dealt with self-esteem issues. Last year was the hardest time in my life. I had an eating disorder from December until October of this year. I almost committed suicide because of all the negative things I said about myself. I have dealt with so many bad things throughout my life, and I was fed up with it.

The first time I found out about Operation Beautiful was when I was looking for quotes online about being beautiful. I started crying because it made me feel regret and shame about the things I did, and I knew I had to make a change in my life. Everyone saw the struggle I was going through and helped me go down the right path to stop it. I started putting Operation Beautiful notes everywhere, and I've posted about three hundred sticky notes all over Texas and Nebraska. I just love seeing people's reactions to these notes!

Today, I live a healthy life and have stopped my eating disorder and my negative talk thanks to Operation Beautiful.

Alexis, Texas

I posted these notes because I wanted to spread the self-love craze that's sweeping the Western world into my own country. I want our mindsets to be about healthy choices and not what you look like or what you do. When it comes down to it, if you love yourself, then you're more likely to treat yourself right with healthy choices. This doesn't mean being a perfect eater or never having fun—this means knowing what you, your body, and your mind need, and what's right for you! I posted these notes in Taiwan. An approximate translation would be, "Make a healthy choice today. Tomorrow, make another. The day after, make another. The day after that . . . you know what to do!"

Wei-Wei, China

Meagan, Wisconsin

The most beautiful woman I know is my mom. Besides being beautiful on the outside, she is also the most special, kind, and loving woman I've ever known. She has four children, but she somehow manages to take care of everyone and lets every kid know how much she loves them. I can testify that her love is unconditional. I'm fifteen, but I've been struggling with my body image for many years. She was always by my side. I don't think I'll ever be able to thank her enough for everything she did and still does for me. All I can say is that my love for her has become unconditional, too. She'll always be my role model and the most beautiful woman I know.

Gabriela, Brazil

I put up my Operation Beautiful note display in the locker room at the campus gym, took my pictures, and then went to work out. About an hour or so later, I stopped back in the locker room to change and see if maybe anyone had taken one of my notes. I was changing about ten feet away from the mirror that I covered with my signs, and I saw a girl walk up to the mirror, get the biggest smile on her face, take one of the notes, and walk out of the locker room glowing. I couldn't hold it in—tears welled up in my eyes. I got to witness firsthand the impact of one of my Operation Beautiful notes, and I can say without question that it was one of the BEST FEELINGS in the world. I will never forget the look on her face or the feeling it gave me to see such a beautiful moment.

My mission is to help other people realize that they are worthy, loved, strong, and capable of conquering anything, just as long as they allow themselves to step out of their comfort zone every once in a while. We are all beautiful in our own unique ways, and I hope to help others realize this fact through posting Operation Beautiful notes for the rest of my life.

Sarah, Virginia

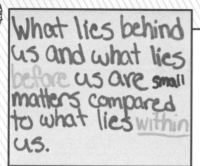
What lies behind us and what lies before us are small matters compared to what lies within us.

I started doing Operation Beautiful notes in the summer of 2010. I loved doing it, and it made me feel so much better about myself when I posted those notes. I have struggled in the past with self-image issues and found posting the notes helpful to all my negative thoughts.

In August of 2010, my boyfriend Jordan and I went to the mall. I was on a mission to buy the first Operation Beautiful book and post notes. Jordan was an amazing sixteen-year-old boy, and he was supersweet. We sat down in Barnes & Noble after I bought Operation Beautiful, and I started making more notes. I felt him staring at me, and I looked up at him, expecting him to joke with me about how I was silly for doing this. Instead, he looked me into the eyes and said, "You are amazing." The last Operation Beautiful note I posted was on that day in the mall. Jordan even posted some notes with me, too. Unfortunately, they were his last Operation Beautiful notes.

On November 6, 2010, Jordan died in a car accident. I have lost my best friend, and the boy I was in love with . . . Jordan was one of a kind, and he was the most caring person I've ever met in my life.

About a month after Jordan passed, my friends could tell I was really struggling and snuck into my room and posted Operation Beautiful notes all over the place. When I returned, I found over thirty-five notes posted throughout my bedroom and bathroom. Every note was beautiful. I cried reading every single note. It meant so much to me. I've realized through this all that my life is full of amazing people. I have friends that are there for me to help me through this.

Later that evening, there was a beautiful sunset. One of my best friends Marissa (who was part of posting notes in my room), took a cell phone picture of it and messaged me with "Jordan painted you a picture." But I realized later that the picture wasn't for me . . . that beautiful sunset was for Breanna, Shelbi, and Marissa. Jordan was thanking them from heaven for doing a beautiful thing and making me smile.

Katherine, Minnesota

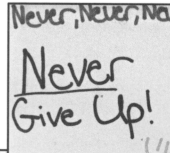
Never, Never, Never Never Give Up!

Your Beautiful Mind: Inner Beauty

This section is about the truest, deepest form of beauty: confidence! We'll talk about how the focus on the way we look can chip away at our self-esteem. You'll also begin to learn how you can boost your confidence by focusing on what an amazingly unique person you are on the inside.

The True Meaning of Beautiful

"I want to be described as the girl who believed she could, so she did," says Emily-Anne, a sixteen-year-old from Virginia with shoulder-length, brown hair and a big, wide smile. Emily-Anne is the kind of girl that you wish was your big sister—friendly, fun, and caring.

Just being in Emily-Anne's presence makes you feel all warm and happy inside. It's like a little bit of her confidence rubs off on you just by talking to her. "When I was ten, I remember reading a quote that said the best revenge is massive success, and I never forgot it," she says proudly. "Standing out and being different

instead of trying to be 'normal' and fit in is important to me."

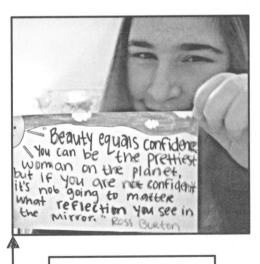

"Beauty equals confidence. You can be the prettiest woman on the planet, but if you are not confident, it's not going to matter what reflection you see in the mirror." Ross Burton

Emily-Anne, Virginia

Emily-Anne was born with an extra bounce in her step, but she admits to having "good days and bad days," just like anyone else. "My insecurities were rooted in my fear of what others thought about me," she remembers. Because she wanted so badly to be accepted, Emily-Anne wouldn't always do or say what she really wanted to.

"When I was in middle school, I would avoid hanging out with certain girls because they were hated by the popular kids," admits Emily-Anne. "I was afraid if I was seen with them, I would receive the same treatment from the more popular kids. Once I got to high school, I stopped caring about who I hung out with and chose real friends instead, but during middle school I very much feared what others would think of the people I surrounded myself with."

Word Up Teen-Esteem

You can't see it or touch it, but self-esteem is the most important thing you own. When you've got lots of self-esteem, you're more likely to try new things and talk to new people. You believe in yourself and your abilities. You appreciate your unique inner beauty!

If you're lacking self-esteem, you might feel like nothing you do is good enough. You might have trouble forgiving yourself when you make mistakes or feel uncomfortable trusting other people.

Teen-esteem is a special kind of self-esteem that only kids like *you* possess! Teen-esteem is unique because it has a powerful impact on your friendships, your achievements in school, and even what kind of adult you'll grow into.

Friends, teachers, parents, coaches, and outside influences like the media or your religion can shape your teen-esteem, but in the end, you're in control of how much self-esteem is in your possession. And although you can't buy self-esteem in any store, you can create more of it. This book is bursting with simple ways you can boost your teen-esteem and become a happier, more confident person.

As she got a little older, Emily-Anne realized it was completely within her power to increase her self-esteem. Inspired, she turned to the Internet to help other tweens and teens find their inner beauty, too. She created a nonprofit organization called WeStopHate (youtube.com/user/WeStopHate), a group of girls and boys from all over the world that creates online videos to spread a message of self-appreciation and "teen-esteem." "Our goal is for teens across the world to love themselves for who they are and have the confidence to stand out in a crowd," says Emily-Anne. Hundreds of thousands of tweens and teens have viewed the dozens of videos, which are created by kids their own age and encourage everyone to love their unique personalities and bodies.

Running the YouTube channel has helped Emily-Anne fully realize that being beautiful has nothing to do with looks. "I think someone is beautiful when they are selfless and kind. To be beautiful, it is essential that you help others and work to bring something positive into the world," she observed. "Yes, I think I am beautiful, because I am doing my best to better the lives of others, while also staying true to myself."

This is exactly what Operation Beautiful is all about—that true beauty is something that resides in our hearts, not on our skins. When someone scribbles "You are beautiful!" on a Post-it and sticks it on a bathroom mirror, in a locker room, on a magazine cover, or on a random car windshield, they're really talking about *inner beauty*.

✸ Do It Now! ✸ Give a Compliment

Giving someone a compliment is a great way to boost their self-esteem; however, it will only have a positive impact if the receiver truly believes what you say. A great compliment is specific and sincere, such as, "Mom, I really appreciate how you always take the time to pack my lunch." You can directly give someone a compliment, or you can send them a compliment in an e-mail, text, or even a handwritten note or letter. The best kind of compliments focus on inner beauty, so try complimenting someone on their personality instead of their pretty shirt!

Not only do compliments make the receiver feel nice, but they also boost the giver's self-esteem. Nothing feels as good as making someone else smile!

Inner beauty is hard to define because, like self-esteem, it's not something you can see or touch. You can't measure inner beauty or bottle it up. Inner beauty is part of what makes humans . . . well, *human*. Inner beauty is compassion, kindness, a willingness to try things, and a desire to include other people so no one feels left out. Thoughtful actions—like when you trip and spill a bag of groceries and a stranger helps you pick everything up—are beautiful. Love is the truest expression of inner beauty, which is why you probably think your mom, favorite teacher, youth group leader, or best friend is beautiful. Inner beauty is a special kind of magic that every person carries inside them.

Love is the truest expression of inner beauty.

Operation Beautiful isn't about what you look like, how much you weigh, what kind of clothes you wear, or who your friends are. Operation Beautiful is all about celebrating and expanding your own unique inner beauty. The most important thing in life is your character, which is determined by how well you treat yourself and other people.

Inner beauty is a special kind of magic that every person carries inside them.

When someone smiles at you and you can tell they really mean it, doesn't it just make your entire day? A big, cheerful smile makes you feel so welcomed and happy. You immediately want to get to know that person better. That's because their awesome inner beauty is showing on the outside! On the other hand, do you know someone who is physically pretty but is not a good friend, cheats at school, or is rude to strangers? She might be pretty, but her character doesn't draw you in. Her lack of inner beauty takes away from her outer beauty, doesn't it?

The most important thing in life is your character, which is determined by how well you treat yourself and other people.

People with a strong sense of inner beauty and character are the most beautiful people of all. You have this magic inside of you, too!

I was really scared to give presentations when I was in middle school. It was always a huge fear of mine. My knees would shake, my voice would tremble, and my thoughts would become nothing but a jumble. My fear of public speaking stemmed from my lack of confidence. I always thought people were judging me. I overcame my fear slowly. I began to realize that mostly everyone in the classroom probably experienced the same feelings I did.

I realized that when I overplanned a presentation, it did not go as well. When I spoke naturally and from my heart, I was able to get my message across. I had always believed that being vulnerable was a bad thing. Each presentation got easier, and I gained confidence and came to realize that even the best speakers do not know the answers to everything; however, they are genuine and honest.

Now, twice a month I give presentations at various high schools and middle schools across Long Island about self-confidence and eating disorder awareness. If someone told me in middle school that public speaking was going to be such a huge part of my life, I would have never believed them. When I stand up there, now as a nineteen-year-old, I feel powerful. My voice makes a difference. I learned that I have important things to say and do. When you feel strongly about something, speak up. Every voice counts! Whether the fear is big or small, accomplishments bring the feelings of excitement, passion, and the confidence to know that you can do anything you set your mind to! All you have to do is believe!

Liana, New York

Meagan, Wisconsin

Many times in life things will get you down. Having someone in your own corner can get you through anything. When your biggest fan is you, there is nothing you can't overcome.

Debra, New York

In seventh grade, I had really bad acne. I would walk through the hallways and get called "pimple face." No one ever wanted to be around me, and I was always left out of groups. It hurt, and I would never pay attention in class because I was always so depressed. I had to work really hard at the end of classes just so I could barely pass. I was even put on antidepressant medicine. During the middle of the year, I learned that I had ADHD (attention deficit hyperactivity disorder). Kids began to make even more fun of me because I was in special education. I felt like I couldn't handle it anymore.

Then, I got invited to go to my church's Confirmation and Youth group. I became very active in my church group and was put on medicine for my ADHD and acne. My acne cleared up, and my ADHD wasn't as bad. I became less sad the more active I became with my church group, and I started helping the orphans in America, Kenya, and other parts of the world. Fewer people were bullying me, and my grades started getting better.

In eighth grade, I was named Class Clown of the Year. It might partly be my ADHD, but I'm a naturally funny student, always cracking jokes and having fun. A little bit later, I was introduced to Operation Beautiful. I started posting notes around my school, and it gave me a big sense of accomplishment. I felt like I was making a difference. That's been my dream for a long time—to make a difference.

Anya, Nebraska

The Beauty Myth

"All right, Operation Beautiful," you may be thinking. "I agree that inner beauty is the most important thing. But come on—outer beauty is important, too, right? If it isn't, why does it seem like everyone in the world is so focused on it?"

It's true—our world is *really* obsessed with outer beauty. If you need proof, just turn on the television or open a magazine. It's hard to ignore the fact that everyone selling this stuff kind of looks . . . well, exactly the same. Sure, some models or celebrities might be blondes and others are brunettes, but most celebrities fit a certain mold: Most are thin, have perfectly straight and white teeth, and wear lots of makeup and expensive clothes. How often do you see a celebrity rockin' jeans and a T-shirt with her hair pulled up into a ponytail and her glasses on? Not very often at all! All this glitz and glam sends a clear message: If you want to be attractive, you should try to look as much like these models and celebrities as possible.

Take a closer look at what those models and celebrities are selling. You'll be bombarded with advertisements for products that promise to make you "better." There's makeup to make your eyes look brighter and face wash that rids your skin of pimples. Cell phones, watches, toys, and even DVDs are sold in ways that try to convince you that you'll be cooler if you own them. If you stop to think about it, our entire culture is focused on buying stuff with the end goal of making ourselves prettier and—apparently— happier. Except no one seems very happy for long, do they? There's always something else to buy or some new way to "fix" our appearance.

> It's true—our world is *really* obsessed with outer beauty.

✦ Do It Now! ✦ Recharge Your Inner Beauty

Between school, friends, sports, extracurricular activities, chores, and trying to squeeze in enough sleep, you probably feel like you don't have enough "do nothing" time. Life can get superbusy! Here are ten ways to take some time out, relax, and recharge in ten minutes or less.

1. Paint your nails a fun color.
2. Take a bubble bath or a long, hot shower.
3. Read a chapter of a book.
4. Grab your iPod and listen to your favorite songs while walking around the block.
5. Do some slow, gentle stretches—they will loosen up your muscles and relax your mind!
6. Write an old-fashioned letter to one of your grandparents.
7. Look at old photographs of your friends or family.
8. Clean your room or organize your datebook. Some people actually find this relaxing!
9. Lay on your bed, close your eyes, and do some breathing exercises— breathe in and out slowly, concentrating on making your inhales as long as your exhales. This is one type of meditation, which is similar to prayer. During meditation, a person sits or lies down, stays very still, closes their eyes, and relaxes their mind and body. A person who is meditating might repeat a positive mantra over and over again in their head, pray to God if they are religious, or visualize (pretend) that they're in a very relaxing place, like the beach.
10. Play with your pet. Studies have proven that petting a dog or cat actually lowers your blood pressure (a physical sign that you're feeling stressed out)!

Somewhere amid all the stuff and fluff, we've forgotten about inner beauty. It's like a veil has been pulled over our eyes and we can't focus on what really matters. A lot of people—both kids and adults—feel very unhappy when they look in the mirror. Because of all the negative messages in the media, we might feel like we can never measure up to some invisible ruler of what's pretty and cool. We feel like we cannot possibly be good enough because we don't look like so-and-so and we don't own the hot, new purse.

As a result, tweens, teens, and adult women are experiencing a serious national confidence crisis. This means we're afraid to speak up and be our true selves because we don't fit exactly into the mold that society is selling. This lack of self-esteem is taking away from the most important thing—our inner beauty. Just how bad is this crisis?

- A total of 81 percent of ten-year-olds say they are "afraid" of being fat.
- A girl is bullied every seven minutes in the school yard, playground, stairwell, classroom, or bathroom.
- The number one wish of girls aged eleven to seventeen is to be thinner.
- Women make significantly less money compared to men who do the same job!
- Boys are five times more likely to receive attention from teachers and eight times as likely to call out in class. Overall, boys talk three times as much as girls do in classroom discussions.

Fast Fact: Girls are more afraid of becoming fat than they are of nuclear war, cancer, or losing their parents.

So, yes—it's true that many people in this world focus on outer beauty. And some people judge your worth by what you look like. But they're just wrong—the truth is that outer beauty will not win you any best friends or help you ace a test. Outer beauty doesn't cure diseases or stop wars. Outer beauty doesn't feed the hungry or rescue homeless animals. Outer beauty cannot experience true love. Emily-Anne, who created the WeStopHate YouTube channel, is the perfect example of someone who is changing the world through inner beauty and confidence. Girls like this—like *you*—are the future of this world. Together, we can rediscover our inner confidence and change the focus from outer to inner beauty.

Journal It: Truly Beautiful Characteristics

Think beyond physical appearances—what makes someone truly beautiful? Let's create a list of beautiful qualities.

- A good listener
- Tells the truth
- Kind to strangers

What else? Write your ideas down in your Operation Beautiful journal!

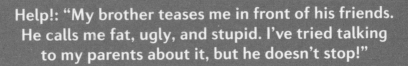

Help!: "My brother teases me in front of his friends. He calls me fat, ugly, and stupid. I've tried talking to my parents about it, but he doesn't stop!"

Some people try to take advantage of those who they perceive as weak or a "people pleaser." A people pleaser is someone who bends to other people's wills and puts themselves in inconvenient situations to help other people. While it's awesome to be flexible and helpful, people pleasers take it a little too far, allowing others to walk all over them.

Standing up for yourself is hard, especially when you need to stand up to a close friend or family member. Standing up for yourself isn't about being bossy or rude; it's about asserting your right to be treated with respect. It's difficult to understand how someone who is supposed to love you can treat you so badly. The secret is that their negative behavior isn't necessarily about *you* at all; they are merely directing their own feelings of low self-esteem at you. Some people think they can make themselves feel better by treating others harshly.

The first step is to talk to an adult about the situation. If your brother still mistreats you when your parents are out of sight, it's time to take matters into your own hands.

Your tone of voice and body language say a lot in these situations. If your brother starts to tease you and you draw inward, hang your head, and whisper, "Please stop," he's probably not going to stop! This is called being passive. The other extreme is being aggressive, which is when you might shout, "I hate you!" or throw something at your brother. Being aggressive is just as ineffective as being passive because it puts the other person on the defense and makes them act more aggressively, too.

> **A people pleaser is someone who bends to other people's wills.**

Help! (cont)

Reacting in an *assertive* way might stop the behavior in its tracks. Assertive behavior is confident and straightforward. An assertive way to respond to your brother would be to pause and think before you react. Take a deep breath, stand tall, look him in the eyes, and calmly say, "Mom has talked to you about bullying me before. It hurts my feelings, and I would not say these things to you. I don't deserve this type of treatment, so I'm going to leave the room."

Above all else, remember that no one can make you feel inferior without your permission. Don't give bullies the permission to treat you badly and make you upset. You can choose to react to the hurtful words with indifference. Walk away and keep your head held high!

When I first got braces I was terrified. I did not like that it looked like a fence running through my teeth, and I didn't like that they were so tight. But now I like that my teeth are getting straighter. I also like that the dentist lets me change the colors of the bands! Braces are the accessory of the year, I think.

Linsey, Missouri

I have struggled with feeling inadequate in the past, which started when I reached middle school. Those years are so difficult; everyone is changing both physically and emotionally. There is a lot of pressure to be perfect and to match up with the "standards"—pretty, smart, and talented. Because of this, I always felt like I was not enough and that I needed to change. For me, it came in the form of an eating disorder, trying to control what I looked like on the outside. However, I am learning that I have always been enough, I am enough, and I always will be enough. I am learning to see myself in the image of God and that I am exactly the way He wants me to be. There are things that I simply cannot control and change, and I need to just let go and LIVE!

Anonymous, Arizona

God grant me the serenity to accept the things I cannot change; courage to change the things I can; and the wisdom to know the difference.

Mackenzie, Indiana

Always remember how AMAZING you are! SMILE!!
www.operationbeautiful.com

Ruby, Ohio

At twelve years old, I wanted to be a popular girl so badly it hurt. I wanted to be friends with those girls. I wanted one of those boys to like me. I wanted to wear clothes that all those girls wore, which all those boys liked to see those girls wearing. For me—at age twelve—that meant clothes from Limited Too, the place to shop. I came home from school one afternoon to find Mom at the kitchen table with a T.J. Maxx bag. She pulled from the bag two Limited Too silk blouses. Up until this point, my collection of Limited Too apparel had been spotty—a plaid shirt, a pair of shorts, a sweatshirt. Two expensive-looking silk blouses, though? This was big time. This was it. Those girls were going to like these Limited Too blouses. And those boys would notice me because those girls noticed me. I was going to be popular.

I wore one of the blouses to school the very next day. I remember walking from English class to the cafeteria feeling like this was it. This blouse was it. I was it. Until I heard it . . . laughter. I was fussing with one of the nylon straps of my backpack when it broke the hallway's silence. I looked up from my backpack's strap thinking nothing of it. I discovered a pack of those boys standing in a classroom's doorway laughing at something in my direction. My face felt warm immediately. The ivory, cinder block hallway ahead of me morphed into that bizarre *Twilight Zone* tunnel. "They can't be laughing at me," I thought. "Please don't be laughing at me," I cringed to myself. I ground my back teeth nervously.

"Nice shirt," one of them said as he threw his head back in laughter. I looked around me. There really was no one else in this hallway. He was laughing at my blouse. He was laughing at me. If it wasn't a deep enough cut to feel when you're twelve, he threw in a biting conclusion. "I think my mom has that shirt." He and his friends laughed. I bit my lip to fight back tears, walked to the nearest bathroom at the end of what was now the longest hallway in the world, locked the stall's door behind me, sat on the toilet, covered my mouth so no one would hear, and I cried. I cried so hard.

I wish I could say that after fifteen years I struggle to remember this experience. Truth be told, I remember it as clearly as if it happened yesterday. I can still feel my head turning to the left to look at the pack of those boys. I can still name the specific boy who threw those insults my way. I can still see the bathroom's artificial light hitting my pants as I hung my head and cried. I can still feel that hurt of realizing not only that this blouse was not going to make me popular, but also there was now a void of wonder and anxiety as to what I could do to be popular—to be liked. Looking back on it now—at age twenty-seven—I think I remember it so vividly for its irony—my desire to be popular with that crowd left me alone, crying privately in the bathroom, which was the exact opposite of what I was after in the first place. What I came to realize years later was that the popularity does come. But it doesn't happen when you're doing their thing. It comes when you're doing your thing. That's it.

Meg, North Carolina

Sixth grade is the first year we were able to try out for cheerleading. Five of my best friends and I made the squad. I had been watching the cheerleaders and wanting to be one of them since kindergarten; now it was my turn. I was superpumped and optimistic. But just one short week after making the team, we were fitted for our new cheerleading uniforms. When we were getting fitted, the representative from the company called out our measurements for her assistant to take down. Most of the girls' height and arm and waist numbers were very similar. Then, it got to me. The whole room heard that my numbers were a lot bigger than everyone else's. My friends hadn't realized how much bigger I was before this. I don't think they were trying to be mean; they were surprised that I was the same age as them but such a different size. I felt like a giant. And I hated it.

From then on I started to become hyperaware of how I was different from the other people in my class. For a very long time, I tried to squeeze into shoes three sizes too small so my feet wouldn't look so big. I avoided my friends when we changed together so they wouldn't accidently see the size of my shirts. I wished on every star that I would wake up one day with dainty, little hands and feet and a body to match.

It took a long time for me to realize that just because I am different doesn't mean it's wrong or bad or ugly. I've slowly learned how to use my differences to my advantage. I was a vital member of our cheerleading squad because I was strong and able to hold my friends in stunts. We won a huge regional competition and probably wouldn't have been able to if I couldn't help hold my friends up in the air!

So my friends and I can't share shoes, and my bright-red hair sticks out in a photograph—now I see that it's really not a big deal. My friends and family don't care about those things. Their love really is "one size fits all." And that fits me perfectly.

Monica, California

Turn Your Negative Thoughts Around!

Whether you're bashing your looks or abilities, mean words can really hurt your confidence. Get ready to learn how you can become a more positive thinker, even on the days that you feel totally down and out. Positive thinkers make the world a more beautiful place!

Whatcha Fat Talkin' About?

Fat Talk is one of the most common types of negative self-talk. Despite the name, Fat Talk isn't limited to the feeling of being "too big" and it has nothing to do with your actual size or weight. Fat Talk is about what you look like (or think you look like), but it's more about how you feel about yourself on the inside—like you're not good enough because of your appearance. Fat Talk can be targeted at any part of your body: eyes, ears, legs, arms, tummy, butt, or even your teeth. Fat Talk is about your body being "too much" of something—too big, too small, too round, too flat, too crooked, too straight, too curly, too tall, too short, too unique, too plain, too light, too dark, or too hairy!

Fat Talk can be targeted at any part of your body: eyes, ears, legs, arms, tummy, butt, or even your teeth.

Word Up Fat Talk

Fat Talk is negative noise about your body. Fat Talk can be internal or external. This means you can have Fat Talk thoughts that you keep to yourself (internal) or you can also speak your Fat Talk out loud to other people (external). The trouble with Fat Talk is that it adds up over time and negatively influences the way you see yourself—as well as how other people view you.

If you struggle with negative self-talk, take the **Fat Talk–Free Pledge**. Make it a personal goal to try and go one day, one week, one month, or even one year without Fat Talk. If you catch yourself Fat Talking, replace your negative thought with a positive and realistic thought instead.

Think about the last time a friend was Fat Talking. Perhaps she was complaining about her "too wide" shoulders or "too frizzy" hair. Did you roll your eyes or shake your head in disbelief because it's so obvious that she's being overly critical of herself? Any outsider could see that she was just nitpicking—plus, she's such an amazing friend, so *who cares* if her hair frizzes up when it rains! Your friend was focusing on this minor physical flaw because Fat Talking has very little to do with what you actually look like.

> Did you roll your eyes or shake your head in disbelief because it's so obvious that she's being overly critical of herself?

You heard right—Fat Talk is really about how you *feel* about yourself. We often put ourselves down when we feel nervous, sad, mad, or bored. Sometimes, we'll even talk badly about ourselves in the hopes that someone will tell us, "No, no! You are so wonderful!" (This is called "fishing for compliments" because you're literally using your negative talk as bait for praise!) The trouble is that fat is not an emotion. When you say, "I feel so fat!" but you really mean, "I feel really lonely at my new school," you are covering up your real emotions. By bottling your feelings up and smothering them in Fat Talk, you're damaging your self-esteem. This kind of Fat Talk is like a wall that you put up between yourself and other people. How can people get to know the true you if you Fat Talk instead of sharing your deep-down thoughts?

Fat Talk can also just be a bad habit. You might not even realize what you're saying when you Fat Talk! Perhaps you Fat Talk so much that it's part of your daily ritual; for example, when you get ready to go to school, you might try on three different outfits and Fat Talk to the mirror.

How can people get to know the true you if you Fat Talk instead of sharing your deep-down thoughts?

Additionally, Fat Talk can be a *social norm*. A social norm is something that society expects you to do in certain situations. For example,

shaking hands to introduce yourself to a stranger at a party is a social norm. Fat Talking is such a part of our culture that other people might expect you to do it! A friend might Fat Talk about her appearance and wait for you to also say something negative about yourself. Some girls consider body-bashing to be a type of bonding experience because it's almost like sharing secrets.

When you are constantly bombarded by Fat Talk, it's hard not to integrate those statements into your own thought patterns. ("If *she* thinks she's ugly, what do other people think of *me*? I'm so disgusting!") Sometimes people Fat Talk in social situations so others will say their Fat Talk isn't true and give them a compliment.

Journal It: Flip Your Fat Talk

Do you find yourself struggling with negative self-talk a lot? Create a positive script (a plan of what to say or think) so the next time you catch yourself Fat Talking, you can replace your Fat Talk with positive talk right away!

"If you are surrounded by people who are constantly criticizing their own appearance or others', it can be hard to remember that there is an alternative way to look at the issue—that appearance is really not the most important thing in life," points out Dr. Joy Jacobs, a clinical psychologist who specializes in self-esteem and body image issues. "This is especially true if tweens and teens have grown up hearing their parents routinely criticize their own appearance."

Not only is Fat Talk a twisted sort of conversation starter, but many girls and women Fat Talk to make other people like them! That sounds strange, doesn't it? But imagine that you're sitting in class and whisper to a girl that you're just getting to know, "I feel like such a pimply freak today!" The girl might feel bad for you and smile sympathetically because she can relate. Now imagine that you said to the girl, "I look superhot in my new jacket, don't I?" This is not a social norm and she might wonder, "Who does this girl think she is?"

While Fat Talk might be a social norm, it can have serious consequences. Fat Talking hurts your self-esteem, which messes up your ability to get along with other people, try new things, and make healthy choices. Because it's contagious, your Fat Talk might make someone else feel badly about their body, too.

Changing your thought patterns takes work, but your Fat Talk is entirely within your control. Here are some easy ways to begin to eliminate Fat Talk from your life:

- When you catch yourself Fat Talking, make a point to correct yourself. That means you should acknowledge your Fat Talk statement and remind yourself that it is a type of negative noise.
- Flip your Fat Talk around! Replace your Fat Talk statement with something that is positive and realistic.
- Ask yourself why you just engaged in Fat Talk. Look closely at the situation and decide if you Fat Talked out of habit, to deal with an emotion, or because it was socially expected. Are you under a lot of stress? If so, you might be Fat Talking as an outlet for your stress; however, there are healthier ways to handle stress, such as exercise, talking to a friend or parent, or writing in your journal.
- If you Fat Talked to deal with an emotion, find a positive and healthy way to handle your feelings. You might want to write in your journal or blog, text or call a friend, or talk to someone in your family about your problems.
- If you engaged in Fat Talk because it was socially expected, correct yourself out loud if it's appropriate! For example, if you just asked your friend if you looked fat and realized you were Fat Talking, laugh and say, "I don't know why I just asked you that! I know I look fine." This way, you'll not only undo the damage the Fat Talking did to your own self-esteem, but you'll also minimize the effect it has on other people.
- Post an Operation Beautiful note for a stranger to find!

Help!: "My mom Fat Talks all the time. When she's cooking dinner, she goes on and on about how she can't eat something because she doesn't 'deserve' it since she skipped the gym that night. We go shopping together and all she does is pick herself apart. She is an awesome mom, and her Fat Talk drives me crazy!"

As you examine your own experiences with Fat Talk, you might realize that you picked up this language from your mom or another woman (or even a man!) in your life. Fat Talk is not just limited to tweens and teens. Grown women and men Fat Talk for all of the same reasons that tweens and teens Fat Talk: It's a social norm, it covers up troubling emotions, and it's a habit. Furthermore, just like it's hard to go through puberty, it's often emotionally difficult to deal with the physical changes that occur naturally during the aging process.

Another major reason you, your friends, or your mom might Fat Talk is the **Thin Ideal**. The Thin Ideal is the idea of beauty that the media has created over time through pictures in magazines and commercials on television—for example, that women should all be skinny with straight teeth and silky hair. This ideal is extremely unrealistic and impossible for most women to obtain, which can increase body hatred and Fat Talk. The Thin Ideal is discussed in greater detail in a section called "Selling Beautiful."

Fat Talk: It's a social norm, it covers up troubling emotions, and it's a habit.

If your mom engages in Fat Talk, take a moment in private to ask her if she's aware of her Fat Talk. It's helpful to say, "Mom, when you Fat Talk, it makes me feel . . . because . . . ," so she knows the impact her words have on other people. For example, "Mom, when you Fat Talk, it makes me feel uncomfortable because I think you're the most wonderful mother on the planet!" Share what you've learned about the causes of Fat Talk, as well as the impact it can have on self-esteem. Ask her to take a Fat Talk–Free Pledge to help each other minimize and eliminate negative noise. You can even post Operation Beautiful notes around the house to remind each other not to Fat Talk.

"Mom, when you Fat Talk, it makes me feel uncomfortable because I think you're the most wonderful mother on the planet!"

Remember that Fat Talk can be the expression of someone's self-esteem, and the reasons for low self-esteem can be very complicated. "Ultimately, it may not be possible to change someone else's self-talk and may require a decision that it simply is not healthy to discuss certain topics (like appearance) with certain people," advises Dr. Jacobs.

Meera, Ohio

She's pretty, but you are gorgeous! Don't judge yourself on how others look.

EMBRACE YOUR UNIQUENESS!

operationbeautiful.com

When I asked myself what I didn't like about my body, I had to laugh. My legs, my hips, my arms, my stomach, my face, my butt; the list goes on and on. I have always been the biggest girl in class. These are not notions that we are born with, though. These thoughts stem from what we are bombarded with every day, whether it be through the media, family, school, and even our friends. This type of thinking, not only from myself, but also the people around me, is so horrible for you.

Most magazines make it seem like the only body type that can be considered beautiful and sexy are the thin, tall ones with big boobs. It is rare that you see a woman with a blemish or of an average weight. "Beauty" sells, not reality. We need to realize that every one of us is different. If we can believe that some people can be smarter than others, or more creative, then why can't we believe that beauty comes in all shapes and sizes?

I'm slowly beginning to realize this, and I hope other people can, too.

Katie, Ontario, Canada

I'm thirteen years old. I like the way I can shrug things off and take everything in stride. I've learned not to take other people too seriously because I know their meanness or rudeness comes from somewhere else, and I'm just their outlet.

Rhy, Georgia

THE MIRROR does NOT define you.

beauty is NOT a size

intelligence is NOT a number

YOU are STUNNING & STRONG!

BUT MOST OF ALL, YOU, (yes, you) ARE

beautiful

www.operationbeautiful.com   www.givesmehope.com

Fat Talk was all around me and my friends. My friends did it, moms did it, and nobody really stopped to think how all the negativity affected people. I always compared myself to the models in magazines and the celebrities on television—I would pick out all the things that made me different from them and feel as though I wasn't as pretty. I think the media definitely had a lot to do with my own negative thoughts about body image. There were no plus-size models in the magazine ads, and it was still considered a bad thing to be anything but a sample size. Although I think media still has a long way to go in changing the social norms surrounding body image, it is good to know that small changes are happening. In the end, it's about feeling healthy and good about yourself no matter what size you are.

Ashleigh, Michigan

My mom is the most beautiful woman I know because she has always been there for my two older brothers and me. She is a kind and loving woman and takes care of everyone else. My love for her is unconditional, and she'll always be my role model. Sometimes I hear her talk badly about her body, and it hurts to hear that. I always tell my mom that she is beautiful inside and out, every way, shape, and form! And to always think on the positive side, too!

Veronica, Michigan

Other Types of Negative Noise

Some people think that their thoughts really aren't that big of a deal at all—they're just little statements that only exist in your own head. No one else even hears your thoughts. Millions of random thoughts race through your brain every day. Thoughts really aren't that important, right?

Think again! One of the most interesting—and scary—things about thoughts is how powerful they can be. Pretend you're wearing a new, white skirt, and your dad serves spaghetti for dinner. As you look down at your plate, one thought echoes in your head, over and over: *Do NOT drip spaghetti sauce on your new skirt. Do NOT drip spaghetti sauce on your skirt. Do NOT—Ahhh!* What did you do?! You spilled spaghetti sauce all over your skirt. Or pretend you're walking across a stage to accept an award in front of your entire school. *Do NOT trip and fall. Do NOT trip and fall. Do NOT . . .* yep. You guessed it. You tripped and fell.

Our thoughts have the power to become reality. If we worry about something negative happening, we increase the odds that it will happen. If we focus on positive things, we create positive energy. Sound a little far out there for you? Well, try this example on for size: Let's say it's your first day at a new school, and you decide to repeat a positive mantra (also known as a message) whenever you feel nervous. Your mantra is: "I feel friendly and excited, and I know that I will find some great, new friends." As a result of this thought, your entire face will look friendlier, and your body language will be welcoming. Other students will be more likely to approach you. If you had negative thoughts racing through your head ("Everyone is going to hate me!"), you might walk around with a scowl on your face and your arms crossed defensively across your chest. No one will want to say hello because they'll think you're the new, mean girl!

Fat Talk about your body is easy to recognize, but it's not the only type of negative noise. People engage in negative self-talk about all sorts of things: their personalities, relationships with other people, school or job performance, and even their intelligence! Just as Fat Talk damages your self-esteem, negative self-talk in all of its forms is harmful. Negative thinking also increases stress, which makes everything seem that much harder.

Psychologists have identified many different types of negative thinking; the list below is just the tip of the iceberg of the complex way people can think negatively about life. Do you engage in any of these negative thought patterns?

- **All-or-Nothing Thinking:** This type of negative thinking involves seeing everything as either good or bad. Also called "polarizing," all-or-nothing thinking means you are only pleased if everything went exactly to plan—which, of course, it rarely does because life just doesn't work out that way! When one thing goes wrong, you tend to see the whole situation as a complete failure and waste of time.
- **Should've, Could've, Would've Thinking:** Constantly obsessing over how things could be different is another type of negative thinking. While it can be productive to examine your actions, second-guessing yourself constantly can be exhausting—plus, once something is done, it's done!
- **Mind Reading and Fortune-Telling:** No one can read minds, but a lot of us pretend that we can—"She canceled our movie night! She must hate me!" Mind readers often assume that others are thinking badly of them, even though there isn't proof. Another type of negative thinking that is closely related to mind reading is fortune-telling, which is when you negatively predict what bad things are going to happen.

- **Catastrophizing:** A catastrophe is a large-scale disaster, like an earthquake or flood. When someone engages in catastrophizing, they assume the worst-case scenario will occur. This thought process blows everything negative out of proportion. "I did so poorly on that test that I'm going to fail the class, and then I'll never, ever get into college" is one example of catastrophizing because one test in one class won't impact whether you get into college.
- **Filtering:** A filter is a device that lets some things in while keeping others out; it's like how you can purify water to remove toxins by running it through a filter. When you engage in negative thought filtering, you only "hear" negative things that other people say and ignore their compliments. If you had a great dance recital and won second place but can't stop thinking of how one judge said you need to practice more, you're filtering.
- **Me-Me-Me Thinking:** Assuming that it's always your fault when something bad occurs is a type of personifying. You might struggle with feelings of guilt or anxiety.

Fast Fact: Be Real!

A 2009 study showed that excessively positive self-statements (such as "I accept myself completely!") can actually backfire in people who already have low self-esteem because these statements jump-start extreme negative thinking (like "No, I don't! I hate my body and have no friends!"). This is why it's better to replace your negative thoughts with something positive and realistic—you have to believe yourself! The next time you're filled with negativity or self-doubt, try thinking, "I know I'm not a perfect person, but I do my very best and appreciate the effort I make."

You've probably heard someone say, "I am under so much stress!" and then let out this great, big sigh. Stress is anything that causes you to worry or feel nervous, like a big test, changing schools, or fighting with your best friend. Did you know that stress can be caused by happy things, too? If you were promoted to captain of your soccer team, it might be a source of good stress because you have more responsibilities.

Signs you're under stress include trouble sleeping, tense muscles (usually in your back), stomachaches, headaches, feeling sad or being easily angered, skin problems (like acne), changes in appetite, or an increase in negative self-talk.

Negative thinking can be triggered in two ways. First, an incident might occur that makes you think negatively. If you get a test back with a bad grade on it and this causes you to catastrophize, the test is the direct cause of your negativity. However, sometimes negative thoughts occur without any immediate cause at all. You can think of these random negative thoughts as "popcorn thoughts" because they pop up out of nowhere. (The proper name for popcorn thoughts is "automatic negative thinking.") If you got a decent grade on a test but spend the rest of the day thinking, "I should've gotten an A . . . I am a total failure . . . I'm never going to pass this class . . . everyone must be laughing at me behind my back," your thoughts have become popcorn thoughts.

> You can think of these random negative thoughts as "popcorn thoughts" because they pop up out of nowhere.

You can work to minimize or eliminate negative thinking just like you can stop Fat Talking. Many of the techniques are the same: First, you want to acknowledge that you are thinking negatively. Then, you want to identify the cause of the thought and whether the thought is logical or makes sense. (For example, "My friend must hate me because she canceled our movie night!" is a clear example of mind reading, and it's illogical because she never said she was mad at you and is really busy with school.) Take a deep breath and replace your negative thought with a positive one.

> ### First, you want to acknowledge that you are thinking negatively.

Also, decide whether your negative thoughts are about something within your control. Sometimes people complain about something that is within their control. If you forgot to study for a test—and that's why you did so badly—promise yourself that you'll study for the next one and move on. Responding to a negative situation in a proactive way (that means you study what went wrong and choose the best course of action to fix it) is a very positive way to deal with disappointment.

Remember that thoughts become actions, and if you want to change your life—you can!

Journal It: My Best Qualities

One easy way to stop negative thinking is to make a list of all your positive personality characteristics. Whenever you feel sad, reread your list to remind yourself that you are unique and beautiful! Try to add something new to your list each week.

Here's an example: *My friends always feel comfortable telling me their problems because I am great at keeping secrets.*

I am twelve years old, and I found out about Operation Beautiful when my mom went to the Girls on the Run summit [GOTR is an international nonprofit organization that works to build elementary and middle school girls' self-esteem through running] in Arizona. She came home and posted Operation Beautiful notes around my room. The notes said all kinds of supportive things. She told me about how Operation Beautiful had helped so many girls.

I decided to post some notes in the girls' bathrooms at school with my mom's help. This brightened my life a little because my parents are not living together anymore, and they have been fighting a ton. I hate it when they fight and am supersad, mad, and just plain unhappy. I wanted to help others who were going through this, too. I hoped my notes would change someone else's life . . . as it did mine.

Annika, Michigan

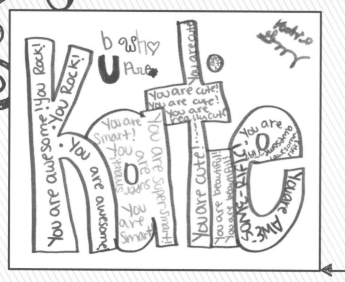

I wrote my name out and then filled in each letter with these phrases because I really think that I am awesome-rific, beautiful, and smart. I really think that it's helpful to write nice things about yourself because whenever you're down, you can just look at these things, and then they make you feel a whole lot better!

Katie, Virginia

Susannah, Virginia

Katie, Ontario, Canada

With confidence, you've **won** before you've even started! BE CONFIDENT! YOU'RE BEAUTIFUL!

operation beautiful.com

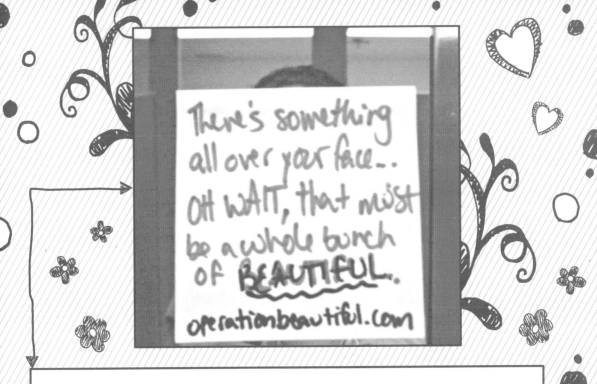

There's something all over your face... OH WAIT, that must be a whole bunch OF BEAUTIFUL.

operationbeautiful.com

College was a huge change for me in so many ways. I'm a fashion major at Drexel University, so I started my three-hour studio classes right off the bat. I have always loved art, and now I finally have the opportunity to take long art classes like I've wanted to for years. The only problem is that they're so much work! It was tough to learn how to manage my time and split it evenly among my art projects, other homework, seeing friends, and just getting enough sleep. I also had to learn to live away from my family and friends—a huge change.

I love college, and although I was terrified at first, I'm learning new things about myself: who I am, what I can do, and what I want from life. Don't be afraid of big changes; changes can be a wonderful experience that will help you grow in ways that you never knew you could.

Estee, New Jersey

I'm sixteen years old, and whenever I'm stressed or sad or anything like that, I write. I write like crazy and just get all my feelings out. Either through poetry or a random paper about something I've been thinking about, I can always express myself. I can write out all of my thoughts and everything on paper, much easier than I can if I'm just talking to someone.

Mackenzie, Indiana

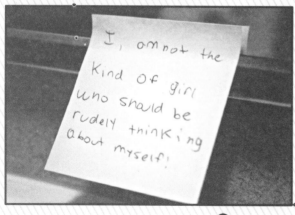

Hope, Ohio

Bullying Isn't Beautiful

Bullying is probably a hot topic at your school because it is one of the worst kinds of negative noise. This section will explore why friends bully one another, what you can do to stop bullies, and how to handle bullies in cyberspace.

Friendship Isn't a Weapon!

Anne's family moved around a lot when she was growing up because her father was in the military. "In second and third grade, I lived in Washington, D.C.," remembers Anne, a friendly blonde with a passion for cooking healthy food. "In D.C., I made an amazing group of friends, and I was devastated when my parents told me we were moving again at the end of the year. I had to leave all my best friends behind; however, in seventh grade, we moved back! I could not have been more thrilled."

Anne's old friends from elementary school were now at the middle school with her, and they threw her a big welcome back party. "I felt like I was coming home again," she says.

But almost immediately, Anne noticed that things were different. A few new girls had joined the group in the years that Anne had been away, and Anne felt shy around them. "A few months into the school year, the new girls decided that, for whatever reason, they didn't like me," she recalls. "And if they didn't like me, that meant no one else could, not even all my former best friends."

> I was devastated when my parents told me we were moving again at the end of the year. I had to leave all my best friends behind.

The other girls began to separate themselves from Anne. One day, she walked into the middle-school cafeteria and sat down at a table with her friends, but everyone stood up, gathered their things, and left without saying a word. All of her friends began to avoid her, even though she didn't do anything wrong. The last straw came when Anne discovered a note in her locker that simply read: *DIE! Nobody likes you.*

"I vividly remember just standing there, staring at the note, reading it over and over again. My heart started beating faster, and I felt the blood rushing to my face. I had no idea what to do. Was anyone watching? Were they waiting for my reaction? Should I just close the locker and leave? The note wasn't signed. I had no idea who had written it, but I figured the new girls were behind it," Anne remembers. "I felt horrible. And betrayed. And I was sure that nothing would ever be good again."

I vividly remember just standing there, staring at the note, reading it over and over again.

When you imagine a bully, do you think of a scary, mean boy threatening to hit someone? Hitting, punching, or physically intimidating someone is direct bullying. The type of bullying that happened to Anne is called indirect bullying, and it's just as real as direct bullying. Girls are much more likely to take part in indirect bullying, which is also known as relational aggression and is most common during middle school and at the beginning of high school.

Word Up) Relational Aggression

Relational aggression is an indirect form of bullying. This kind of bullying is meant to cause damage to someone's relationships and social standing with others. Examples of relational aggression include telling secrets, spreading rumors, excluding, name-calling, or lying. Prank phone calls and mean text messages are also examples of relational aggression.

Your friends form a social circle. Other groups at school have their own circles, too. The circles can overlap if one friend is close to someone else in another circle. There's one big circle that encompasses all the kids in your grade, and another even bigger circle that includes everyone at your school. When relational aggression occurs, the bully harms your reputation in your immediate social circle and maybe even in other circles, too. Girls might do this because they feel threatened, want others to know how socially powerful they are, or are unhappy about something that has nothing to do with their victim—maybe they are having trouble at home, for example. They might even do it for fun or because they are simply bored.

> When relational aggression occurs, the bully harms your reputation in your immediate social circle and maybe even in other circles, too.

While physical bullies use their fists, social bullies damage your reputation by spreading lies, teasing, or creating rumors. They might also blacklist you from the group by refusing to let you sit with them at lunch or no longer inviting you to after-school activities. Social bullies often recruit other members of the social circle to follow their lead; people might do what they say because they are scared to challenge the bully.

It might be hard for others to even *recognize* social bullying. Teachers and parents sometimes wrongly chalk the behavior up to "girls being girls" or "girl drama." Operation Beautiful knows that girls are full of inner beauty and that social bullying is *not* normal girl behavior! Social bullying often flies under the radar of what most adults are trained to watch out for. That doesn't mean that social bullying is painless—in fact, the emotional damage from this kind of bullying can be just as serious as that from physical bullying.

✷ Do It Now! ✷ Become a Better Listener

One way you can minimize the impact of bullying is to strive to be a better listener, not only for your friends, but for other kids at school, too. It's hard for people to reach out for help sometimes, but talking to someone who actually cares can make all the difference to someone who has been bullied. Here are some simple ways you can brush up on your listening skills!

1. When a friend starts to tell you something important, stop talking and put down any distractions, such as your cell phone. Try not to interrupt!
2. Don't think about how you're going to respond while they talk!
3. Be open-minded and don't judge your friend as she shares.
4. Show you're listening with your body—face your friend, uncross your arms, look her in the eye, and nod your head at appropriate times.
5. When it's your turn to talk, summarize what they've said first to be sure you understood correctly.
6. If you feel uncomfortable giving advice because their problem is really big or serious, consider talking to a parent or trusted teacher at school. Sometimes the best thing a friend can do is help a person reach out for help.

When most people think about bullying, we focus on the times we were the victim. But the truth is that someone has to be the bully, and nearly everyone has engaged in bullylike behavior at least once. If you've ever gossiped about a friend, rolled your eyes at someone while they talked, or laughed at someone behind their back, you were engaging in bullying. Bullies are not totally evil people, and the line between being a bully and getting bullied can get blurred. Maybe a friend starts a horrible rumor about you, so you "get back" at them by spreading lies. Or maybe you just sit silently as one friend talks badly about the other. Although you aren't directly bullying anyone, you're adding to the problem by not speaking up against this hurtful behavior!

Word Up) Projecting

If someone is **projecting**, they are subconsciously (which means they do it without realizing it) assuming that someone else has the same feelings and motivations as they do.

For example, let's say there is a girl in your class who always gets straight As and is loved by all the teachers. You also get good grades and are respected by teachers. One day, the girl accuses you, in front of the whole class, of cheating on the math test. She insists that you cheated on the test, even though you didn't, and she has no proof. The truth might be that she actually cheated on the test and is *projecting* her guilt onto you! Another example of projecting is when a social bully encourages a circle of friends to banish one person from the lunch table. Perhaps the bully is actually afraid of being rejected, so they *project* their feelings and cause someone else to be rejected.

The secret to dealing with projecting is to understand that *it's not really about you*. People who project onto other people are dealing with their own complex and unhappy emotions. That doesn't mean their behavior isn't harmful, but understanding projecting is one way you can learn to take things less personally and reduce negativity in your life.

If you're being bullied (physically or socially), the first step is to tell an adult. Talk to your teacher, a counselor, or your parents. If the first adult doesn't help you, tell another adult. Keep telling adults until someone helps you! If the bully is supposed to be your friend, try pulling her aside and privately asking her why she is treating you this way. Try saying, "We don't seem to be getting along lately. How can we work together instead of against each other?" and see how she responds. If you're engaging in bullying behavior, you should also talk to a trusted adult about what you did and how it makes you feel. If you think your behavior isn't that big of a deal, ask yourself, "How would this make me feel?" The best thing you can do is stop the behavior and personally apologize to the person you hurt.

For Anne, it was never too late to hear the apology. Fifteen years after she moved away from the middle school that she had been tormented at, one of the girls—now an adult—e-mailed her after years of silence and asked her out to dinner. Anne agreed to go because her negative feelings about the situation had melted away. "We had a blast reminiscing about old memories, gossiping about what our other friends were up to now, and catching up on each other's current lives," says Anne. "And then, just as we were finishing dinner and drinks, she turned to me and said, 'There's actually another reason I wanted to meet up with you tonight. Do you remember that note in your locker?'"

Anne, Washington, D.C.

"She had asked me to dinner because she wanted to say she was sorry," continues Anne. "She said she has thought about that note often over the years and cringed at the fact that she had done something so horrible. She said she regrets writing it, and that she didn't even really know why she did it. I know that peer pressure and wanting to be cool makes girls do and say stupid, mean things. I don't blame her for wanting to fit in. I know now that she didn't really mean what she wrote. But I didn't know that then."

Bullying is not beautiful! Operation Beautiful believes that all people are worthy of respect. Talk to your friends about social bullying and pledge to stop the toxic behavior together. YOU can change the way girls interact with one another. "And know that you are not alone if you're being bullied. There is always help available," adds Anne. "It will get better. I promise you."

Help!: "I find it really hard to say no to other people. I always end up doing favors for people even if I don't have the time to do so. I feel like a doormat!"

Saying no can be so tough! But letting other people walk all over you is even worse. If saying "yes" too often is stressing you out, it's time you flex your power to say "no thanks!"

The next time someone asks you to do something that you really don't have time for, simply say, "I'm sorry, but I can't do this for you right now because my schedule is so full." Say it nicely, but with a firm voice! Shake your head side to side as you say no; it's been scientifically proven that people accept "no" more easily with an accompanying head shake!

It's best to say no with a simple explanation of why you're refusing—such as "I have a lot of homework this weekend and just don't have the time to help you study." Don't feel like you owe anyone a long explanation for why you can't help; saying you're too busy is a perfectly acceptable reason. Some people are really pushy and ask you more than twice! In these situations, there's nothing wrong with changing the subject or even walking away.

If someone keeps pushing you after you've said no, you can take the pressure off by adding, "Again, I'm pretty sure I won't be able to do that, but I'll think about my schedule a little more and get back to you!" Alternatively, you can refer the person to someone else who might be able to help them—"I can't tutor you, but Sarah is really good at math and might be willing to study with you."

When I stepped on the school bus on my first day of sixth grade, I couldn't have known that the day would set the tone for the next six years of my life. There were four girls who sat in the row behind me on the bus—they were one year ahead of me in school, and they immediately started picking on me. They made fun of everything from my socks and my hair to my facial expressions and my name. The teasing continued on for years, and although it did fade as we got older, it never completely stopped until they graduated and left school. They went so far as to pour hot chocolate in my hair one morning on the bus!

In seventh grade, my P. E. teacher suggested that I, along with one other girl in my grade, try out for the soccer team. I loved playing soccer. But the mean girls played on the soccer team, so I gave up. My mom got involved, the school got involved, but nothing stopped them. My parents told me to just ignore them. For six years, I just blocked them out and tried to avoid them in the hallways as much as possible.

But now that I'm older, I wish I had stood up to them. I wish I had made them see that I wasn't their victim and that they could not—would not—treat me that way. I would've stood tall and walked proudly, confidently. If they made a comment, I would look them in the eye and comment right back. Or, as my mom always said, another option would've been to "kill them with kindness." But I never tried. I always just stayed silent.

I regret that I let those bullies have so much control over my life. They got to choose whether or not I played sports, and they got to choose which hallways I walked down. I'm twenty-eight years old now. The teenager in me still has no idea what I did to make them dislike me. But the adult in me knows that I didn't do anything, and some people need to tear others down in order to lift themselves up. In the long run, being bullied made me a stronger person with a thicker skin, and I am confident in my abilities both as a person and as a woman. And now the only person who gets to make choices for me . . . is me!

Raya, Arizona

In fifth grade, I was bullied. I went from being relatively popular to most of my friends turning on me in a span of just a few weeks. Most of my friends refused to talk to me, sit with me at the lunch table, or pick me for teams at recess or in gym class. I said something to my parents before I said something to a teacher, but my teacher knew something was going on. I was always a straight-A student, and my grades had started slipping.

With girls, bullying usually isn't physical, so it can definitely take the form of verbal abuse, the silent treatment, or spreading rumors online, which can be even more hurtful. My mom and my teachers intervened. Eventually, it just stopped. I was no longer friends with those girls, but I didn't want to be, anyway.

The important thing to remember is that it comes from people who aren't happy with themselves, so they take it out on other people—and that things will get better. Always.

Theodora, New York City

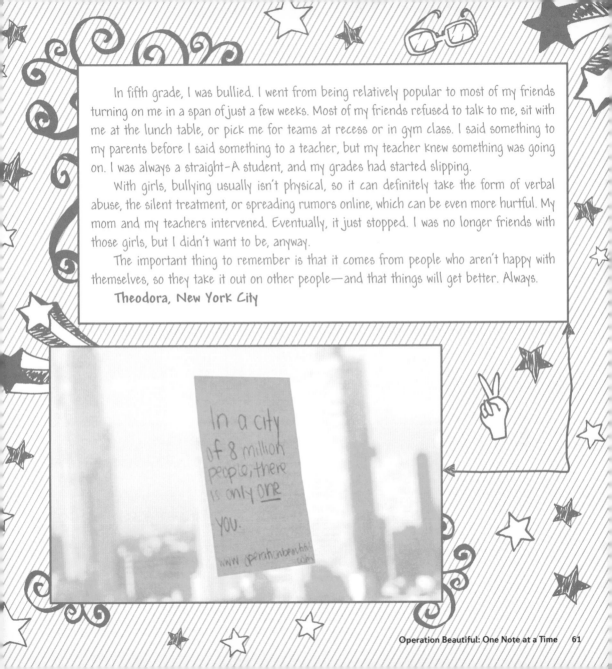

In a city of 8 million people, there is only <u>one</u> you.

www.operationbeautiful.com

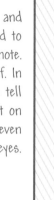

I posted colorful Operation Beautiful notes all over my high school, and then I sat near one for ten minutes as the bell rang and everyone rushed to class. As I sat there, I counted how many people smiled after reading my note. In ten minutes, I made 103 people smile. I never felt so good about myself. In fact, my best friend and I are going to host an assembly at our school to tell everyone about Operation Beautiful. We've made stickers for people to put on their shirts and over one thousand premade Operation Beautiful notes. We even made T-shirts that say, "I am beautiful!" Operation Beautiful has opened my eyes. It's amazing to feel beautiful again.

Livv, Ontario, Canada

you are:
beautiful!
Operationbeautiful.com

Don't worry your life away. Hate is the poison. Love the remedy.

I was bullied by two other boys in middle school. There was this kid in my homeroom who I had gone to preschool with. We became friends and hung out once at his house, but after that, he started acting aggressive, verbally threatening me, and once even grabbing my neck. I spoke to my guidance counselor, and eventually our rabbi stepped in to stop the behavior. Another boy often called me a "fat girl" during lunch. (I was kind of overweight.) I went home crying many times.

I didn't really start to branch out until eighth grade. I think going to a lot of bar and bat mitzvahs in seventh grade helped me to become more social and become friendlier with a lot more people. In eighth grade, I started to connect with my classmates and even got my first girlfriend. We started going out in February that year and lasted for nine months. I also felt more comfortable with my body and personality. Eighth grade was definitely the best year of middle school.

Looking back, I would say that middle school is just a struggle with confidence. Kids should be comfortable with who they are and who they are developing into. Surround yourself with people who are nice to you. Make friends with people who respect you and who you have fun with. It's perfectly okay to leave your elementary school friends, especially if they start to be mean to you. Also, if you're having troubles or issues, please talk to a guidance counselor about it! They're all supernice and want to help you. Let them support you.

Lastly, if middle school seems like it's a never-ending suckfest, just remember that you can totally push through. You can make it through, and I promise you that it will only get better from there. Hang in there. You can totally do this!

Adam, New Jersey

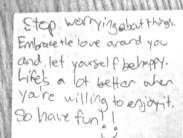

Stop worrying about things. Embrace the love around you and, let yourself be happy. Life's a lot better when ya're willing to enjoy it. So have fun! :)

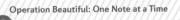

E-Bullying

Bullying doesn't just occur at school—it can also happen online and over the phone. This kind of bullying is called **cyberbullying**. Cyberbullies use chat rooms, blogs, Facebook, or other social network sites to publicly humiliate or harass other kids. E-mail, text messages, instant messages, and direct messages might be used to "trick" someone into revealing a secret.

Many parents can totally relate to kids who are being bullied—but they have zero idea what it feels like to live in the Internet Age as a tween or teen. Back in the day, kids who were bullied prayed for the final bell to ring so they could leave school and get away from the negativity. But now, kids have to face their bullies in person at school *and* electronically on the Internet. They leave school for the safety of their homes, turn on their computers, and are harassed with horrible messages from their bullies.

Cyberbullying can be just as scary and hurtful as real-life bullying. Not only does it tear down victims' self-esteem, but anything written or posted on the Internet lasts *forever* because people might save files or forward e-mails to their friends. Cyberbullying can damage someone's reputation and even hurt their chances of getting into college down the road.

But now, kids have to face their bullies in person at school *and* electronically on the Internet.

Amy was a little shy in middle school, but she liked running and joined the track-and-field team. "I started to become friendly with some of the popular guys because we were running together every day," remembers Amy. Even though they were all on the same team, Amy sometimes felt shut out by many of the track-and-field girls. "I had a collage of pictures in the front of my binder, and a few of the girls in my math class started to tease me, making comments about how the guys weren't my 'real friends' and just 'felt bad for me.' It hurt a lot."

One day, Amy signed online and received an instant message from a stranger with the screen name "AmySmells." "I would receive messages that said, 'You are ugly!' or 'You are just a loser!' or 'Stay away from our boyfriends!'" Amy describes. The messages hurt just as much as any real-life bullying, and the cyberbullying made her increasingly uncomfortable at school. "I felt like I always had to look over my shoulder," she recalls. "The popular group would whisper behind my back and even threaten me in the hallways."

Amy blocked the "AmySmells" screen name, but her tormentors just created new screen names. The cycle of harassment lasted all through middle school. "To this day, I do not know for sure who was sending the messages, but I do believe it was a group of several popular girls," says Amy, now an adult. "I think I was too embarrassed to tell anyone what was happening. I never even told my parents," she says. "I think more girls need to be aware that this happens to a lot of people, and you can get through it. Bullies hide behind the Internet because they have their own self-esteem problems."

Alexis's story is a lot like Amy's. Alexis says her cyberbullying troubles began when she switched to a new school. "It all started last year, in seventh grade. No one knew who I was, and I felt like a complete loner," she says. "One night, I signed onto Facebook and received a message from a girl known as the 'popular girl.' She said all this mean stuff to me, like she didn't even care how it made me feel."

Bullies hide behind the Internet because they have their own self-esteem problems.

"I started to cry like crazy after I read the message," says Alexis, who is now thirteen years old. The Facebook message made her feel even worse about the situation at school and pushed her into a downward spiral of unhappiness. "I kept getting more rude comments and mean posts put on my wall," she describes. The bullying soon spilled over into her real life, too. One girl started a mean rumor about how Alexis was an "emo freak." "The rumor grew and grew," describes Alexis. "Soon, I felt like everyone hated me."

Filled with pain, Alexis started to skip classes, and her grades got worse and worse. "Who knew that one little message on Facebook could ruin my life? It wasn't right," she declares. One day, Alexis decided to take matters into her own hands: "I blocked all the people on Facebook who were being rude. The next day at school, I ignored everything that people were saying. I decided to start over. I made new friends and got involved in sports. I felt awesome and brand new." Alexis even decided to forgive some of the people who had bullied her over Facebook.

Hey! Ü Don't believe what Others say! Why? Because you're BEAUTIFUL! <3

@operationbeautiful.com

Alexis, Texas

☀Good to Know: Bullying from Cyberspace

One in three teens and one in six preteens have been bullied over the Internet! In total, more than thirteen million American tweens and teens have been victims of cyberbullying.

✷ Do It Now! ✷ Change Your Privacy Settings

You have the power to control who sees your online information—the tool is called **Privacy Settings** and is available on all social networking sites like Facebook, MySpace, Webkinz, Club Penguin, FBF Kids, and Whyville. Ask your parent or an older sibling to help you adjust your settings so only your friends can see your profile. Don't accept friend requests, instant messages, or direct messages from people you don't know, and remember that you can always unfriend someone who treats you poorly online.

Check the box that allows you to moderate comments on your wall and enable alerts to notify you if someone tags you in a picture. On your profile, remember that you don't have to fill out every field—talk to your parents about whether you should list your last name, age, or school. Never give out this information to a stranger.

Lastly, be sure to disable features that automatically detect your location and blast it to all your cyberfriends. No one needs to know you're at the coffee shop at 3rd Street and Main!

Start today... With a SMILE! You are BEAUTIFUL!

www.operationbeautiful.com

Amy, Pennsylvania

Words are very powerful, and that's why cyberbullying has serious consequences. Many school districts have passed rules that allow principals to punish students for cyberbullying— even if the cyberbullying occurred on the weekend! Social networking sites might also punish cyberbullies by canceling their accounts and blocking their computer's special address (called an IP address) from using the site. Cyberbullies can even be charged with a criminal misdemeanor under antiharassment laws.

But you can't get help unless you tell someone—so be sure to print out all evidence of cyberbullying so you can prove what happened. "Do not be afraid to tell a parent or teacher," Amy advises. "You could also try telling a friend or a sibling. Adults can help you overcome the bullying." For Amy, keeping silent about what happened to her in school and online was a big mistake. "Now that I'm older, I'm realizing who I am and that I am beautiful just the way I am. Bullies will, unfortunately, always be a part of life, but knowing how beautiful you are takes away their power."

"Do not be afraid to tell a parent or teacher," Amy advises. "You could also try telling a friend or a sibling. Adults can help you overcome the bullying."

Help!: "I'm being cyberbullied!"

If you're being harassed or teased online, you don't have to take it! First of all, as always, tell an adult you trust what's going on. Change your privacy settings so the bully can no longer contact you. Save and print all the evidence of cyberbullying and give it to your parents. Your parents should let your teacher and principal know about the cyberbullying so they can address the issue at school. You should also report the bully to the website directly because cyberbullying is in violation of websites' Terms of Service.

In middle school, I did not feel completely confident in myself. I think one moment that I conquered my fears would be when I chose to not follow in my friends' footsteps. Most of my childhood friends chose sports like cheerleading, volleyball, and basketball, but I chose to play tennis and join marching band. It was not the "cool" sport to do. I was not the most popular person in middle school, but looking back I had great friends who cared about me and supported me. I found some of my greatest friends from marching band.

Bullying and teasing happened in my middle school. It was hard at times to deal with being teased about being different from other kids, but one thing that helped was having friends who supported me. When you have people who love and care about you it helps to make yourself see that you're better than those people who have to pick on others.

Ashleigh, Michigan

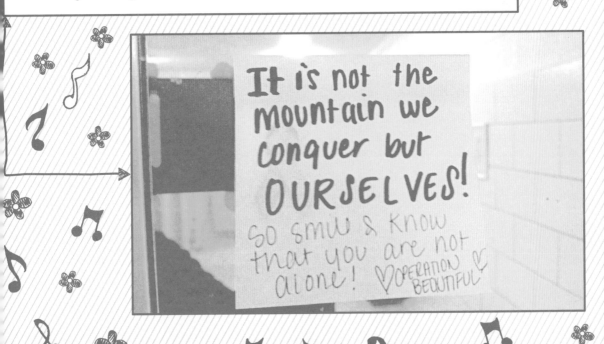

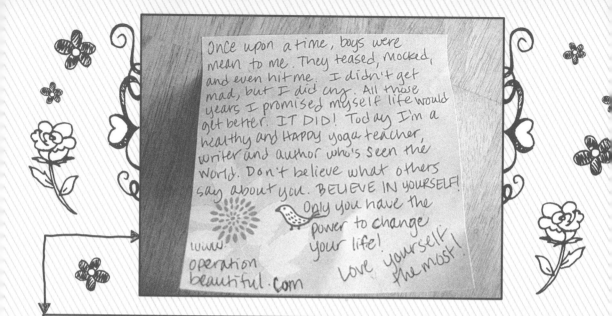

Once upon a time, boys were mean to me. They teased, mocked, and even hit me. I didn't get mad, but I did cry. All those years I promised myself life would get better. IT DID! Today I'm a healthy and HAPPY yoga teacher, writer and author who's seen the world. Don't believe what others say about you. BELIEVE IN YOURSELF! Only you have the power to change your life! Love yourself the most!

www. operation beautiful.com

My family didn't have a lot of money and my home situation was precarious at best (my mom and stepdad divorced, remarried, and divorced again). At 5'10" with long dark hair and pale skin, I was an easy target for teasing. Boys called me names. Girls told me I was ugly and flat-chested. I cried myself to sleep the night before my ninth-grade school photos because a football player barked at me in the hallway that day.

I studied hard and promised myself that I would move away from that small town and all its drama just as soon as I could. I earned a full ride to college, where I double majored in French and journalism, studied abroad, and worked on the school paper. I never moved back to that small town, and my life has gotten better with every passing year.

You and only you can change your life. What people think about you doesn't matter; what you think about yourself does! Hold your head up high, and know that life will get better. You just have to be strong, keep your goals in sight, and be willing to work hard for what you want!

Stepfanie, Ohio

Ever since I was little, I can remember wanting to be friends with the "popular" girls. Sure, I had dozens of friends in every other group, but I really wanted to be invited whenever those girls had a party, went to the mall, or hung out at basketball games. They called me occasionally, but I knew they were really friends with me for convenience. I can remember so many arguments about me being the only one to make an effort. Names were called, tears were shed, but I fought to stay a part of the group. Our grade had only fifty-two students in it, so it often felt like everyone was against me. I can distinctly remember sobbing to my parents and begging them to let me transfer schools. Of course they said no, so I took matters into my own hands.

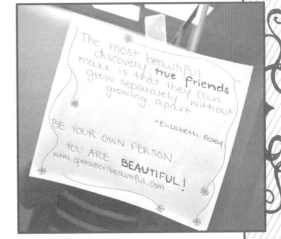

It was just months before graduation, and I wrote a letter to each one of the girls in our group, basically questioning what kinds of true friends treat each other the way we did. I never meant for anyone else to see it, but one of the girls submitted it to the school newspaper without my permission. When I heard it was in the paper, I braced myself for the inevitable backlash, but it never came. Instead, I was praised by students, teachers, and parents for saying what everyone else was thinking. I finished the year without any issues, and I'm happy to say we are still true close friends to this day.

I think many people believe bullying is defined as hurting or teasing someone you do not like: someone "inferior" or "less cool" than you are. However, what I experienced in school was from the people who were supposed to be my friends. We were catty, cruel, and mean. We were friends with someone one day and spreading rumors about them the next. It made some of my middle and high school years the worst of my life, and every day I questioned why I wanted to be friends with people who really didn't care to be friends with me. Without the support of my family (and the guts to write that letter), I really don't know where I would be today.

Allison, Pennsylvania

In school, girls who I thought were my friends turned their backs on me. The cheerleaders I had such a bond with were now the same girls who swore they hated me. The thing about girls is that their attacks aren't necessarily physical or confrontational; sometimes they aim for emotional pain. No one deserves to be the subject of rumors or hurtful words.

The school administration was aware of what was going on but took no real action to stop it. Thankfully, I had people to turn to. I had my family and two of my teachers. My mother and grandmother helped me keep my sanity and strength. I also had my athletic trainer and my government teacher; I admire those teachers because they not only were there for me when I needed to talk, but they also believed in me.

My family and two teachers helped me realize that life isn't about the things that go on in high school or what other people say or think about you. Life is more important than what other people think. You can't let the negative things people say affect the way you view and value yourself. Everyone is beautiful—inside and out—and you can't let negative thoughts overshadow the truth. You are beautiful!

Amanda, Texas

Selling Beautiful

If you feel worse about yourself after reading a fashion magazine, you aren't alone—most people do! That's because the media has a big impact on our sense of self-confidence. This section discusses how the media has shaped our idea of beauty with images of "perfect" models and celebrities. Knowledge is power, and after discovering the truth about the people in advertisements, you might never look at a fashion magazine the same way again.

Marketing Mindfulness

Whenever you watch television, log on to the Internet, drive on the highway, or even sit on a bus, you're probably seeing an advertisement. An advertisement attempts to convince the viewer or listener to buy a product or agree to an idea. Advertisements come in many, many forms, such as television commercials, radio spots, billboards, banner advertisements on websites, signs on street corners, and more. You might even find advertisements on coffee cups! Advertisements are limited only by marketers' imaginations.

Marketers are people who create advertisements as part of their jobs. That's right—there are people who write radio jingles and craft commercials for a living! Most people who work in advertising earned a business degree in college; you can actually major in marketing, which is the study of how to get the public to feel favorable toward a company and, ultimately, purchase the product.

Knowledge is power, and after discovering the truth about advertisements, you might never look at a fashion magazine the same way again.

Fast Fact: Advertisements All Over

Did you know the average tween sees twenty thousand televisions ads each year? Kids less than eleven years old also spend about eleven hours a month on the Internet, where they are constantly bombarded by advertisements and pop-ups. By the time she turns seventeen, the average girl has seen more than two hundred and fifty thousand commercials aimed at her looks!

(Word Up) Media Literacy

Media literacy is kind of like detective work. If you are media literate, you carefully analyze everything you watch, hear, and read to determine if the media is telling the truth or trying to shape your ideas about what's "cool" or important.

The media, which is just a fancy word that lumps together television, movies, books, magazines, and the Internet, often promotes social stereotypes. A stereotype is a very general and unfair way of viewing someone or something. For example, many commercials promote the stereotype that women must be thin to be considered pretty, which is not true. Instead of accepting commercials as you see, hear, or read them, think about the hidden messages that marketers are sending out. Are they trying to make you feel a certain way so you'll buy a product?

Marketers use advertisements to sell products, but they don't just rely on the product's awesomeness to convince people they need to buy it! Marketers try to create an atmosphere, or feeling, around a product so when you see the product, you *feel* a certain way. They do this in a very indirect way and play on our emotions so the messages are more likely to sink in.

Let's say we're a team of marketers, and we have to figure out how to sell a new shampoo. Our shampoo makes hair bouncy and shiny, like most shampoos do; however it's $2 more per bottle than the average shampoo. When we create our shampoo commercials, we need to convince shoppers that our product is more than just plain old shampoo— if you use our shampoo, you'll be prettier, more confident, and have more friends! Our commercial will feature a woman with supershiny hair dancing and laughing with her pretty friends at a party. Sounds fun, right? Heck yes! By creating this atmosphere around the product, people who see our commercials might think that our shampoo can not only give them nicer hair, but also a better life. Maybe a girl who just moved to a new area will see the action-packed party in our commercial and feel a little sad because she doesn't have any friends in her new town yet. As a result, next time she's at the store, maybe she'll ask her mom to buy our shampoo instead of the regular, cheaper kind. Our commercial sold not only shampoo, but ideas about popularity and fun. We sold our message to the girl in a very clever way. If we had created a commercial that screamed, "Our shampoo will make you popular," she might have immediately thought, "No, it won't!" Instead, we quietly planted the idea in her head and, when mixed with her own insecurities, the girl came to her own conclusion about our shampoo's worth.

When we create our shampoo commercials, we need to convince shoppers that our product is more than just plain old shampoo . . .

Marketers know that emotions play a huge role in shopping. How many times have you bought something because you thought it would make you happy? How many times have you shopped because you were sad?

Help!: "I want THAT shiny new thing . . . but I'm not sure why! If all my friends have the newest thing, I feel the need to have it right away, too, just to keep up with them."

Americans are obsessed with buying stuff. As a whole, our country is very materialistic, which means we place importance on things like clothes, cars, and gadgets. Instead of spending our time volunteering, playing with our brother or sister, reading books, or just enjoying all the wonderful things we already have, we spend a lot of time focusing on the *stuff* we don't own.

Everyone's family is different. Some people spend a lot of money (regardless of whether they can really afford it!); some families are not materialistic and prefer to save their money or donate extra money to charity.

Materialism is not a good thing. People work very hard for their money, and there are lots of important things to spend it on (food, health insurance, college educations). Materialism makes people spend their money on things they don't actually need instead of saving money or spending it in more useful ways. And while buying things might make you happy for a little bit, the truth is that this type of happiness quickly fades.

The next time you want to buy something, ask yourself why you want it so badly. Did a commercial influence you? Do all your friends have the toy? Do you think the product will make you more confident or popular? Did you see the product in a television show or movie? Marketers use a trick called product placement to subconsciously motivate us to buy things. Marketers will literally pay television shows money to film the main character drinking their beverage or using their cell phone with the brand clearly displayed!

Materialism is not a good thing.

Ask yourself, "If I buy this product, would I have to borrow money from my parents or can I totally afford it myself?" Don't spend money impulsively; go home and sit on your decision. If you really want the product the next day, then you can decide to go back and buy it. Also, is there a better way to spend your money or your parents' money? There are so many charities that need extra funding, and even ten dollars makes a huge difference—and you'll remember your donation a lot longer than you'll like that new shirt!

Thinking about your purchases helps reduce your materialism and refocuses your attention on what's truly important: inner beauty, not *stuff*.

Most people go through daily life without consciously acknowledging all the advertisements around them. However, that doesn't mean that we aren't absorbing the messages! Because there are so many advertisements out there in the world, the messages that marketers send to us shape our perception of what is important. Unfortunately, many marketers are going to try to convince us that we aren't pretty, smart, or fashionable enough so we buy their product! Advertisements send the message that we must wear this makeup, we must wear the best clothes, and we must have the coolest technology. If advertisements told us we were good enough the way we are, companies would go bankrupt because no one would feel like they had to buy their products! When we hear the message that we aren't good enough over and over again, we start to believe it, and this crushes our self-esteem. Did you ever think about advertisements in this way before?

The most powerful message that marketers send us is about beauty. Many people in today's society believe that, in order to be attractive, women should be thin and men should be muscular. This is called the **Thin Ideal** and the **Muscular Ideal**. (An ideal is the perfect version of something.)

If you watch commercials on television or flip through a magazine, you can easily see that marketers usually place value on women who are very thin. Some real-life women are naturally thin, but female models and celebrities often diet their way to a level of thinness that is actually *unhealthy* and puts them at risk for lots of different diseases due to their low body weight. These models and celebrities are also shown in a way that makes it look like they have no pimples, perfect hair, smooth and tan skin . . . they have no flaws! The ideal man is portrayed as muscular (with "six-pack abs") and tall, with a thick head of hair, perfect teeth, and no blemishes on his skin. Although having muscles is a good thing (for both women and men), sometimes people will take steroids, a chemical that forces their muscles to grow very fast and can cause many health issues. It's important to realize that the ideal of perfection presented in commercials is often unhealthy—for both women *and* men. While commercials show the Thin Ideal and the Muscular Ideal as something to work toward, the reality is that those models and celebrities are often hurting themselves to look a certain way.

❋ Do It Now! ❋ Sneaky Advertisements

Curl up on the couch and turn on your favorite television show. Instead of just watching the characters, pay attention to the products the characters use. Look for clear shots of brand names, such as a close-up of a cell phone screen that says Sprint or a television screen that reads Sony. Maybe the star of the show is drinking a can of Coke or a Starbucks coffee. Commercials don't just happen during the breaks; they occur *within* the program, too. Marketers pay television shows money to include these shots in their shows—how many product placements can you spot?

Fast Fact: Boys Feel the Pressure, Too

Body image issues aren't just a girl problem—boys feel the pressure, too! Boys might feel like they are too big, too short, or not muscular enough. They might look at men's magazines and worry about their bellies or smaller biceps. Common puberty issues such as pimples, facial hair, or deepening voices might cause boys to stress out as well.

The problem with the message of the Thin Ideal and the Muscular Ideal is that most people don't look like this—plus, we can make ourselves very unhealthy trying to look that way! We have curves and bumps, pimples and freckles, frizzy hair and crooked teeth. These things aren't imperfections— they are just part of being human! Just like we created a positive feeling in our shampoo commercial, marketers use the Thin Ideal and Muscular Ideal to stir up emotions in potential consumers. When we see commercials with images of perfect people in them, we might start to believe that those products can help make us "perfect," too.

(As a side note, did you know most of the models you see in magazines and commercials don't even actually look the way they are portrayed? That's because marketers use computers to make the models appear picture-perfect. We'll talk about this more in a bit!)

✳ Do It Now! ✳ Magazine Sleuthing

To do this fun activity, you'll need a paper, a pen, and a magazine aimed at teenage girls or women, like *Seventeen* or *Teen Vogue*. On the paper, write the

❋ Do It Now! ❋ Magazine Sleuthing (cont)

following categories across the top and draw lines between them to create columns: Appearance/Looks, Dating/Boys, Fashion/Makeup, Self-Esteem/Emotions, Family/Friends, Health, School/Career, and Other. Read through the magazine and categorize each article under one of the topics by making a tick mark. Articles can fall under more than one category. For example, if the article were entitled "Find the Best Dress for Your Body," you'd put a mark under the Appearance/Looks and Fashion/Makeup categories.

Once you categorize all the articles in the magazine, you can figure out how often each topic is addressed in the magazine. First, add the number of articles in each category. Then, add the total numbers for all categories to figure out how many articles were in the magazine. Create fractions by putting the first number over the second number. If there are fifteen articles about Fashion/Makeup and forty-five articles in total, you should write the fraction for Fashion/Makeup as 15/45. That's the short way of saying that fifteen out of forty-five articles were about Fashion/Makeup.

On average, articles in tween and teen magazines are mostly about Appearance/Looks, Dating/Boys, and Fashion/Makeup. In fact, these topics are the focus of more than one out of every three articles in a tween or teen magazine! Issues such as Self-Esteem/Emotions, Family/Friends, and School/Career are addressed much less frequently.

What types of articles does the magazine seem to focus on? Do you think magazines for tween and teen girls should focus on other topics?

Extra Credit: Go back through the magazine and count the number of advertisements you can find! How does the number of articles compare to the number of advertisements? How many pages would the magazine be if there were no ads?

Maybe you're thinking, "Okay, so I know all about commercials. But I don't actually *believe* any of those messages they send me! I know they are just trying to sell stuff." The truth is, even if you think you aren't being affected by these messages, you are. Advertisements can find ways to worm into our brains and change the way we think! The impact of seeing these "perfect" bodies in magazines, TV, and online is often subconscious, which means that they quietly affect the way we think about ourselves and perceive other people over time.

"We know that females who compare themselves to their peers and especially toward models in the media tend to have worse body image and self-esteem," says Dr. Dense Martz, a psychologist and researcher who specializes in the study of Fat Talk. "We've become a bit brainwashed in what is real and what is not."

Seven out of ten girls say they want to look like a character on television—but 69 percent of TV actresses are underweight! Three out of ten girls admit that they feel pressure to have the perfect body from the media. And most women (68 percent) say that they feel bad about themselves after reading fashion magazines. Constantly looking at photographs and seeing commercials that depict girls and women as the Thin Ideal has made us very dissatisfied with the way we look. Because we're constantly comparing ourselves to the Thin Ideal, 75 percent of healthy-weight women think they are overweight, and 90 percent of women overestimate their own body size!

The truth is, even if you think you aren't being affected by these messages, you are.

Are you surprised about the sneaky impact that marketing has on the way we think about life? Do advertisements shape your concept of beauty? What important aspects of true beauty do commercials and advertisements rarely portray?

Sometimes I wish I could dress differently. Right now, my style is "whatever I pull out of my dresser." This style of clothes I wear is not complimented on by the other kids in my seventh-grade class, but every once in a while I am complimented by a stranger, which is nice! I also try to tell myself, "You look nice in this shirt today." I don't wear makeup, either. I don't think makeup makes you who you are. Some people get into the habit of always wearing makeup, even on the days they're just lying around the house because they're sick! Perhaps they think they look ugly without it. But the thing about makeup is that you're beautiful without it. You can use makeup to express yourself, but don't let it make you feel badly about who you are.

I post notes all over school because I want others to know about Operation Beautiful. Every time I post a note, it disappears the next day, and I don't know where they go. But there was this one time when everyone was passing something around in my math class, and I saw someone flash this pink note in the air. It was mine! I got this fluttery feeling, and I get so giddy when someone talks about the notes positively. No matter if some of the kids say it's stupid, I am fueled by the people who talk about how cool it was to find the note! I hope more people will pass it on.

Paige, Maryland

I think just about everyone I know has spoken badly or negatively about themselves. I think they say it partially for people to tell them that it's not true and partially just because it has become such a habit to be negative. It makes me feel a bit sad that my friends and family can't see that all their "imperfections" make them beautiful.

I'm sixteen now, but growing up, I felt super self-conscious about my freckles. Now I realize they're truly beautiful and it's part of what makes me . . . me. My favorite thing about my personality is that I can always find beauty in people and things. I believe everyone is beautiful in their own way. The most beautiful women I know are my best friend Maria and my mom. Maria has just always been there for me, and she has a great personality. She's just all around a beautiful girl. My mom has gone through a lot, and she still has a really positive outlook on life. That's one thing I really admire about her.

Morgan, Wisconsin

When I was little, I was made fun of for my weight (I have always been a little pudgy), the little things I did, and for just being there. Later, it changed form, including some harsh words and friend stealing. I've managed to stay happy and be optimistic always, but I am always saddened by how girls in this generation have so much pressure put on them to be the perfect person and, as a result, feel the need to be mean to others.

Two years ago, I was friends with a girl who went to the same summer camp as I did. She was mellow like Jell-O. We would always hang out and come up with the best private jokes in the world. Then, after camp ended and school started, she changed. She put on lots of makeup and constantly talked about her "reputation" and her "superhot" boyfriend (a new guy every week). She kept drifting further and further away. One day, I told her we would miss her at summer camp if she didn't come, and she replied with a "sucks for you." I haven't talked with her since.

I have become so bitter toward the media that tells girls like her that they have to be skinny, wear makeup even if you don't need it, and have hot boyfriends in order to have friends. I am fourteen now and currently looking at high schools. I fear that high school will bring back the world of hate and bullying that I just recently escaped from. There is one thing I know for sure, though: I will ALWAYS be optimistic. I will never degrade myself, tell myself I'm not good enough, or anything like that. I will be happy, always.

Ali, Massachusetts

Many girls at our high school struggle from image issues. There's a lot of name-calling and just plain hatred going on every day. So many of the girls don't even realize how beautiful they are, and it's hard for them to accept compliments because they're always wondering if it's a lie or joke. We've posted notes twice at our school. The first time, we waited until second period, went to the bathroom, and splattered the walls with colorful notes. For the rest of the day, we overheard so many girls talking about how much they loved our notes and considered our mission a success!

The second time we posted notes, it took us weeks to prepare because we wrote so many notes. We arrived at school early and plastered notes all over every bathroom. But by lunch, someone had taken down all the notes in two of the bathrooms. We don't know if they didn't like the notes or loved the notes so much that they decided to keep them. However, later that day, we heard some of the other girls talking about how adorable our notes were. If we made at least one girl feel beautiful, then we achieved our goal.

Brenna, Lilac, and Allyssa, California

Images Don't Equal Reality

The media shapes our perceptions of what is valuable and desirable, which is a big problem for three reasons. First, advertisements are trying to make us feel certain ways so we'll buy their products. Second, advertisements make us focus on outer beauty instead of inner beauty. Lastly, many images in the media are computer-generated or computer-enhanced, which means many girls and women (and men, too!) are striving to look like someone who doesn't even exist in real life!

> ### Fast Fact: Unrealistic Ideals
> Most fashion models are thinner than 98 percent of American women.

That's right—most images you see in magazines and television commercials aren't real! Marketers use a computer program called Adobe Photoshop to manipulate images to make them look "better."

Photoshop isn't necessarily a bad invention; it is often used by photographers to merely "clean up" an image. The photographer uploads the photo into the Photoshop program and uses tools to blend, blur, erase, lighten, or darken parts of the image.

Wedding photographers might use Photoshop to erase a booger in a bride's nose! The photographer can also use Photoshop to combine two images. A baby photographer might combine a photograph of a baby sitting on a blanket with another photograph of the family's dog sitting on the same blanket. By Photoshopping these two images together, the final image will make it look like the dog and baby were sitting next to each other, a practically impossible photograph to coordinate in real life because the puppy and baby would be playing the whole time!

Photoshop isn't necessarily a bad invention; it is often used by photographers to merely "clean up" an image.

The problem with Photoshop is that the program can transform a photograph of a normal-looking person into an impossibly perfect person with a few strokes of the keyboard and clicks of the mouse. In these scenarios, Photoshop is often used to make models' legs appear thinner. They will erase portions of their thighs and hips, sketch in ab muscles on their stomachs, and blend away cellulite and pimples. Photoshop can stretch necks, elongate legs and arms, and make hair appear thicker. Photoshop can even change your hair, eye, and skin colors!

People who are very talented with computers can also manipulate moving images; these are called Computer Generated Images (CGIs). Lots of movies feature CGI special effects. The dragons or giant spiders in *Harry Potter* aren't real, of course—they are CGI. CGI isn't limited to crafting mythical beasts; people can also use CGI to manipulate people in commercials. For example, the lovely, thick hair in most shampoo commercials isn't real hair or even a wig—it is simply CGI effects! No wonder the hair in commercials is always so pretty, right? It isn't even hair that exists in the real world!

Fast Fact: Unrealistic Ideals

To see real examples of Photoshopped beauty, check out operation beautiful.com/photoshop.

✯ Do It Now! ✯ Spot a Photoshopped Cover

The majority of images in magazines have been Photoshopped; however, most are changed in very small ways so it's not obvious. The next time you're standing in line at the supermarket, look over the covers of the glossy women's magazines to see if you can spot little examples of Photoshopping. Sometimes you'll catch a major mistake, like an extra finger or a leg that is twisted in an impossible direction!

Check out the covers and ask yourself the following questions:

- How old is this celebrity or model? Does her skin show her age or have wrinkles been erased? If she's smiling, there should be little wrinkles around her mouth and eyes, no matter what her age! Wrinkles are the natural result of crinkling your eyes when you smile!
- Do her hips look impossibly small or narrow, like a curve has been erased? Most girls and women's hips naturally jut out because of the hip bone.
- Does her skin "glow"? There is a tool in Photoshop that allows the user to enhance skin tones.
- If the model or celebrity is wearing a bathing suit or shorts, can you see any cellulite? Cellulite is a natural dimpling of the skin; most girls who have gone through puberty have a little on the back of their thighs, regardless of their weight.
- Does she have any pimples or blemishes on her skin? Most people have a few!
- Does the photograph of the celebrity make her look thinner than you've seen her in other images, like on television shows or in the movies?
- Do her eyes or teeth look unnaturally bright? Photoshoppers often make blue eyes seem unnaturally blue or teeth appear extra white.

The problem with these kinds of Photoshop images and CGI effects is that it creates a false sense of reality. When you look at an advertisement, you might think, "Wow, that model is so pretty. She is so lucky that she is so tall and thin!" The trouble is that the model doesn't even look that way in real life—she has been Photoshopped to appear taller and thinner!

The problem with these kinds of Photoshop images and CGI effects is that it creates a false sense of reality.

We've been hit with a double whammy by the media! The first blow is that the media overly focuses on the very small percentage of real-life girls and women who fit into the Thin Ideal and men who fit into the Muscular Ideal. The second blow is that marketers Photoshop these already unusually thin or muscular models and celebrities to make them even *more* thin or muscular. They Photoshop models and celebrities so all signs of being a real person are erased: no pimples or stray hairs, no lumps or bumps, no crooked teeth or birthmarks.

Many regular people feel like they are unworthy in comparison to images in the media. Girls might go on unhealthy diets or overexercise in attempts to be as thin as the women in the media. People might worry about it so much that they become sad or anxious. Some people would do almost anything to look more like the media's ideal of beauty—a goal which is impossible because *the images aren't even real.*

They Photoshop models and celebrities so all signs of being a real person are erased: no pimples or stray hairs, no lumps or bumps, no crooked teeth or birthmarks.

How serious is the Photoshopping problem? You can safely assume that every cover and almost every single image—not just the advertisements—in a magazine has been altered in some way by a computer. In particular, advertisements for beauty products are usually heavily Photoshopped. For example, an advertisement for anti-wrinkle cream might feature a model that is your mom's age; however, the model's natural wrinkles have been Photoshopped away so she looks as young as you!

"Wait a second!" you might be thinking. "Isn't that lying?" Yes—it is! But there are no laws about using Photoshop in advertisements, so some marketers use the program to make their product seem more effective. A person who sees the anti-wrinkle cream ad might look at the model's smooth face and think, "Wow! That stuff really works." This is called *deceptive advertising.*

But now you know the truth! There is no sense in trying to look like the images you see in magazines and on television. The Thin Ideal and the Muscular Ideal are just made-up concepts. Instead of making yourself miserable trying to look like something that doesn't even exist, why don't you try to be the healthiest, happiest version of *you*? This is what Operation Beautiful is all about!

Journal It: Fake Beauty

The next time you're flipping through a magazine and spot an example of Photoshopped beauty, cut out the image and paste it in your journal. Use a red marker to circle the Photoshopped parts. Look for necks that seem too long, legs that are too thin, hips that are impossibly narrow, and faces without any wrinkles or blemishes. It helps to remind ourselves that the images presented in the media are not necessarily reality.

The other day I was listening to an entertainment show about celebrities without makeup. The journalist was nitpicking every single one of them, even though they looked perfectly fine to me! It is sad that our media is centered on beauty. I am a junior in high school, and I face beauty issues all day. It is a small school, but there is still pressure to look a certain way. My school is filled with beautiful girls. The pressure for us now is so much more than our mothers faced. We talk about our thighs, stomachs, and hair . . . it never seems to be enough for some. Even between classes I see girls redoing their makeup. I have a very unique head of hair; it's curly and coarse. When I see celebrities, their hair doesn't match mine. It just gets so overwhelming.

I know God created every single one of us differently. I want to share with other girls that they don't have to fit the mold. Our lives are too short to please someone else. That is why I love Operation Beautiful!! Everyone is beautiful. We are so much more than the number on a pair of jeans or the size of a shirt. Beauty is so much more. I posted this note in my school's bathroom. I saw one girl read it. She walked out smiling, which totally made my day!

Justine, Illinois

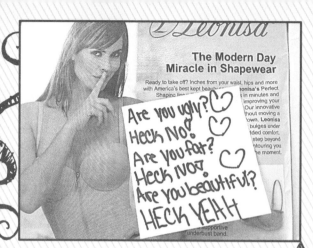

Madi, Ohio

Allie, Ohio

Operation Beautiful is truly amazing; I'm thirteen years old and I love it. I left this note on a car windshield. Operation Beautiful is something we should do every day, not to receive something back for doing it, but to get that warm feeling in your heart because you know you're helping someone! Beauty is only skin deep; it's what's on the inside that counts.

Olivia, Pennsylvania

I posted this note in the front of a copy of the first Operation Beautiful book at my local Barnes & Noble. If I could go back to my tween/teen self, I would tell myself that I can't control other people, but I can control my actions and my responses. I spent a long time comparing myself to others, and that's a battle that nobody will ever win. Once I realized how pretty darn great I am, those feelings of inferiority and not feeling good enough started to go away. Sure, I have my moments of doubt (who doesn't?!), but remembering that I choose how I am impacted by this doubt brings me back to a positive place.

Jessica, Florida

The True You

At this point, you might be imagining that I'm a "free spirit" who refuses to use beauty products. You might think I wander around in pajamas all day long because I clearly don't care about fashion or looking good. In all likelihood, I probably smell pretty bad because I skip scented body wash or deodorant, too.

While I won't claim to be the most fashionable girl, I *do* care about my outward appearance in many ways. I wear makeup regularly, shave my legs, dye my hair so it's a little darker brown than it is naturally, and paint my nails. I go to a salon twice a month and get my eyebrows waxed. (Once, I got overeager plucking them all and practically lost an entire brow!)

> **At this point, you might be imagining that I'm a "free spirit" who refuses to use beauty products.**

One day, I sat down and carefully considered all the reasons that I use beauty products. One part of it is that society expects me, on some level, to do "girly" things like care about fashion. This is called a **gender stereotype**. This stereotype is not only part of our culture (parents give their daughters Barbie dolls to dress up and their sons toy trucks to play with in the dirt, for example), but it's also reinforced through advertising and the media. You don't have to fulfill gender stereotypes if you don't want to; it's perfectly fine to be the girl who prefers blue over pink if that makes you happy! A bigger reason that I use beauty products is that I think it's fun! I loved to play dress-up as a kid, and I still love to do it as an adult; I like to put on a fancy dress and go to dinner with my friends. I also like sitting in bubble baths, putting on face masks, painting my nails, or experimenting with makeup. Not all girls like to do this, but I do!

However, beauty products do not make me who I am. I know that *I'm the same person* whether I'm lounging around in sweatpants and a messy ponytail or a cocktail dress and professionally applied makeup. I'm good enough and worthy of love and respect either way.

You don't have to fulfill gender stereotypes if you don't want to; it's perfectly fine to be the girl who prefers blue over pink if that makes you happy!

One not-so-good reason that many girls and women use beauty products is that they don't feel totally confident without them. Some people rely on beauty products and clothes to boost their self-esteem instead of finding other, healthier ways to do so, like volunteering or developing a new hobby. Without beauty products, some girls feel extra shy or nervous. With one swipe of eyeliner, they feel more confident and secure. It's like beauty products are a coat of armor that helps protect them from the outside world. In their eyes, they aren't good enough the way they naturally are—they need to be enhanced or "fixed."

To Jamie, makeup was covering up her true self, and she was tired of it. Now a senior in high school in Oklahoma, Jamie had started to wear makeup in middle school. "A friend told me I looked really weird without my glasses on, and I took what she said to heart so much that I started to experiment with makeup," she remembers. "Just one negative comment really hurt my feelings. Eventually, I couldn't go to school without makeup on because I felt so weird without it."

One day, Jamie was late to school and had to rush out of the house without applying any makeup. She says she felt horrible all day as a result. "It was such a frightening experience for me! I felt so self-conscious. I didn't realize how many issues I had with my own self-confidence until that day," she explains. "So I decided to challenge myself to overcome my fears."

And that's how Jamie's No Makeup Mondays revolution was born.

Carry yourself like a
queen and you'll attract
a king. ♡ ♡♡♡

operationbeautiful.com

Jamie, Oklahoma

Jamie posted a note on her Facebook wall and explained her intentions to her friends: From here on out, she would skip makeup on Mondays (at the very least!). "The first few weeks, it was very low-key," she says. "It took a while to get used to—I would walk through the halls using a jacket or my hand to hide part of my face, scared that someone would point me out and laugh or something crazy like that. Of course, no one did."

Jamie's friends encouraged her mission and began to skip their makeup on Mondays, too. Then, she chatted online with a youth minister that she had met at church camp. The minister encouraged Jamie to spread her No Makeup Mondays mission even further, so she created a Facebook group that eventually grew to nearly three hundred members, including both girls and boys in the Oklahoma and Kansas area.

Makeup isn't "evil," explains Jamie. "Just like clothes, makeup can be a form of art and self-expression. When used like that, makeup is fun and awesome. But sadly, it seems like our society has created such a sick standard of beauty, and makeup is just one way we are all forced to look the same."

Talking to other girls about makeup and spreading such a positive message has helped Jamie realize that true beauty really comes from the inside, not the outside. "I'm not cool with being so self-conscious. I'm not cool with being all paranoid about what others are thinking about. I'm not cool with being so insecure when I'm not wearing makeup," she explains. "I'm good enough the way I am."

✴ Do It Now! ✴ Start an Operation Beautiful Club

If you want to spread the love and share the lessons of Operation Beautiful, you can start a club at your school, church, or temple. An Operation Beautiful club can be about whatever you want it to be, but here are some ideas that have worked successfully for other girls:

- Talk to a teacher or adult about how to start a club. You'll probably need to follow certain school or church rules or complete some paperwork before getting started.
- Declare a special No Makeup Day to encourage other girls to feel comfortable with their natural beauty. Make buttons that girls can wear on No Makeup Day that explain what you're doing; for example, the button could say "Proudly makeup free!" You can also make buttons for boys who support your mission. Those buttons could say something funny like "Inner beauty is hot!"
- Set up a table in the hallway and have other students write their negative thoughts about their bodies on helium balloons with a permanent marker. Once the balloons are filled up, go outside and symbolically release the negative thoughts into the air! Or you could have students write down their negative thoughts on balloons and then pop them, symbolically destroying their negativity.
- Host a bake sale or car wash and donate the profits to a confidence-boosting program for girls, such as Girls on the Run (girlsontherun.org).

Fast Fact: Beautiful Skin

The big secrets to beautiful skin? Getting enough sleep, exercising regularly, and eating healthily will make your skin clearer and brighter—no lotion or face wash can compare! Drinking water—not soda or other sugary drinks—throughout the day helps your skin stay moist and clear. Lastly, washing your face every night with warm water and a gentle cleanser removes dirt and grime, which reduces the odds you'll experience breakouts. No makeup required!

In high school, it took me one and a half hours to get ready for school. And I had a uniform, so it was only hair and makeup! As soon as I was going out the front door, I needed to have makeup on—even to go get the mail or go on a ski trip. I felt like people would judge me if I wasn't wearing makeup, and I thought I was ugly without it. It took me a while to realize that makeup is an accessory to beauty, not a necessity. I'm nineteen now, but I wish I understood this sooner.

Charlie, Montreal, Canada

Makeup does not define how you are.

You are beautiful. Be proud.

operationbeautiful.com

The proudest moment of my tween years was discovering who I really was and what I wanted to do in my future. For so many years I would compare myself to other girls and change every little thing about myself to try and "fit in." Whether it was buying the "coolest new pair of shoes" or dying my hair to look like everyone else, there was always something I wanted to change so I could "fit in." Now that I'm a little bit older—I'm seventeen—I realize that it really didn't matter if I was like those girls or not. I am me and I shouldn't have to change myself to feel better . . . I was finally able to accept who I was and be proud of myself. I was also able to discover my true interests and focus on me rather than focusing on other people. If there is one thing that makes me different, it is my strength, my power, and my belief that I can truly do anything I set my mind to. And I love myself for that.

I think the kind of beauty in magazines is extremely limited. Sure, the women in magazines are gorgeous and some of them have great skin and great bodies, but not everybody is like that. Plus, there is an excessive amount of retouching used to make that model fit the ideal of perfection. I think the beauty industry realizes that the ideal image has gotten out of control,

but at the same time they don't want to risk using "real bodies" and "real women" because we have gotten used to this idea of perfection. We need to realize that the image society has built up is completely unreal—it is unrealistic perfection.

Carrie, London

You Dont have to Wear make-up to feel Beautiful! You're Beautiful no matter What.... www.Operationbeautiful.com

When someone tells me I'm ugly, I believe them because I'm a very emotional person when it comes to my looks. When I don't feel beautiful, I feel like I need to wear makeup even though I'm still in middle school. But I need to remember that I can—and do—feel beautiful without makeup because I'm just being Korea—I'm just being myself. I tell myself that I shouldn't care what some people think about me because I know I'm glamorous and no one can pull me down, not like they used to. At the end of the day, I will still be strong. I will still be myself. I am beautiful!

Korea, North Carolina

Your BEAUTY IS WHO you are not WHAT you wear! www.OPERATIONBEAUTIFUL.COM Join the Beauty Movement!

In December of 2010, we found out about Operation Beautiful. We are twelve and ten years old, but we knew we wanted to be a part of it. We immediately began putting up little Post-it notes in bathrooms, in stores, and pretty much anywhere we went. In January, we decided that it was time to do something bigger than a regular Post-it.

We found HUGE Post-it notes and wrote positive messages on them. Our whole family drove around and hung the signs in store windows at the mall. It feels really good to do Operation Beautiful, and we hope that whoever sees any of our Post-it notes will feel happy and know that they are beautiful.

Rachel and Lauren, Wisconsin

When I was eight years old, I got acne! I had never worn makeup before, but once I got acne, I wanted to wear it to cover up my "imperfections." My mom took me to a makeup counter to buy me products for skincare, but we bought some other things, too. Most other girls my age didn't wear makeup, so I wore it only to parties and put powder on in the morning whenever I remembered. I know you're probably thinking, "Oh my, makeup at age eight?" But I was broken up about this acne. I cried myself to sleep most nights and hated my skin.

Now I'm fourteen, and my acne has never let up. Last year, I found Operation Beautiful, and all of a sudden, all the makeup in the world didn't matter anymore. I still wear makeup and love to play with it—to me it's like painting a face instead of a canvas! But I don't feel the need to wear it as much, and I still feel pretty without it.

I made this Operation Beautiful note out of ice chunks on the driveway; it snowed today, and I wanted to do something nice for people walking through my neighborhood!

Charlesy, Alabama

The Confidence to Be Yourself

True confidence isn't just about accepting the way you look on the outside—it's about celebrating who you are on the inside! This section provides tips on how to embrace your uniqueness and discover your special passions and talents.

Stepping Out, Not "Fitting In"

Self-esteem is hard to describe because it's a magical power that you can't hold or see. One great way to think of self-esteem is to imagine that it's like a garden. When you're feeling good and your confidence is high, the beautiful garden is bursting with colorful flowers. Rainstorms come and go, but they don't ruin your flowers; they just help your self-esteem grow into an even bigger, more beautiful garden. People might try to pluck your flowers, but the stems are strong and thick. It's not easy to destroy your garden.

When you're feeling low, your flowers just won't open up and bloom; the buds stay tightly closed. Rainstorms drench the soil, creating messy puddles that threaten to drown all the plants. This is a metaphor for the way low self-esteem makes you feel: shy, unconfident, and easily overwhelmed. If your confidence is already low, there's a real risk for someone chopping down your flowers. Not everyone lives with the best of intentions, and some people might try to reduce the beauty of your garden to make themselves feel better.

So far, we've discussed three ways that your self-esteem can be negatively impacted:

- your own negative self-talk as well as the negative talk of people around you;
- being a bully and bullying other people; and
- the excessive importance the media places on physical beauty, the ideal of which is impossible to obtain.

Word Up) Flower Cutters

There are two basic ways for people to behave in this world: positively or negatively. Flower cutters are overwhelmingly negative people who attempt to "cut down" other people to feel better than them. Interactions with flower cutters are negative and drain you of energy and happiness. "You are so lucky you can eat that chocolate cake!" a flower cutter might purr. "I would get so fat if I ate that!"

When all these forces add up, it's a natural reaction to think, "I just want to *fit in* and be like everyone else. If I'm different, people won't like me. I just want to be accepted by *everyone*."

Sari, a nine-year-old from Virginia, says she's different because she's Jewish. "Sometimes, I like to be different because I can show my friends new things like dreidels for Hanukkah and matzah at Passover," says Sari. "I even get to miss school for Jewish holidays. I really like that!" Occasionally, however, Sari finds it difficult to have a different religion than her friends and other kids at school. "Some people make fun of me by saying, 'Our holiday is better than yours! Yours is bad.' That makes me feel excluded because almost everyone in my class celebrates Christmas. It makes me kind of sad when everyone talks about Christmas. I'm not trying to be greedy. It's just that I can't talk about Hanukkah with everyone."

If you're stuck on trying to fit in, you probably wish you could change something about yourself that makes you . . . *you*! Maybe you wish you looked a different way and had a different skin color or hair texture. Maybe you wish you were popular or could play sports. Maybe you wish your parents weren't divorced or your family was the same religion as everyone else at your school. If you weren't different in this key way, perhaps you think you would finally fit in and everything would be so much easier.

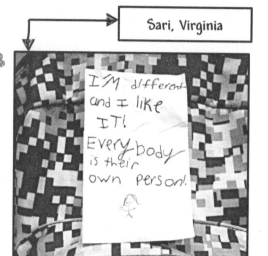

Sari, Virginia

I'M different and I like IT! Everybody is their own person!

Here is a secret: Everyone, absolutely *everyone*, feels like they don't fit in at one point or another! Even the most popular girl at school probably wishes she could change something about her life.

But the truth is that there is only one YOU! The problem with "fitting in" is that you have to lose a bit of your special uniqueness to be like everyone else. If Sari wasn't Jewish, she would miss out on her family's unique heritage and wouldn't get to celebrate Jewish holidays. Sari says she gets to go to Hebrew school where she is learning to speak Hebrew. "I like going to Hebrew school," she says. "I tell my friends at regular school new words in Hebrew and they try to say them!"

Journal It: All the Awesome Ways I'm Different

Instead of hiding our differences, let's celebrate the ways we're unique! Write down a list of the ways you're different than other kids, regardless of whether you normally think the differences are "good" or "bad." Can you put a positive spin on your unique differences? Here are some examples:

Journal It: All the Awesome Ways I'm Different (cont)

I'm different because my family speaks only Spanish at home!

I'm different because I have red hair and freckles.

Help!: "I am so hard on myself. If I don't get an A or if I screw up on a task, I get so upset and feel stupid and worthless. I know it's not the end of the world, but it feels like it is!"

If you are hard on yourself, set goals that you know you can't achieve, and feel very sad when you don't reach those goals, you might be a **perfectionist**. A perfectionist is someone who believes that anything less than perfect is unacceptable. Being a perfectionist can sometimes be a good thing, because it can help people succeed and do well in school and sports. Perfectionists often strive to be productive and meet deadlines, which are very good qualities.

However, perfectionism can take on a life of its own if you're not careful. You might become so focused on getting the details "right" that you lose track of the bigger picture! Perfectionism sets you up for high levels of stress and disappointment because it's impossible to truly be perfect. You might overwork yourself or become very anxious and nervous.

A perfectionist is someone who believes that anything less than perfect is unacceptable.

If you suffer from perfectionist qualities, it's important to remind yourself that it's impossible to be perfect in the first place! Don't fall into the trap of "all-or-nothing" thinking; doing the best you can is truly worthwhile. Another

way you can combat perfectionism is asking others to help you if you feel overwhelmed. Getting assistance isn't a sign of weakness; it's actually a sign of strength because you were smart enough to ask for help when you needed it.

Why would you want to be a copy of everyone else when you could be an original you?

Since perfectionists are often results-focused, take time to enjoy the process of doing something. It's not just the dance recital that matters; having fun with your friends at all the rehearsals is important, too!

Why would you want to be a copy of everyone else when you could be an original you? Instead of trying to hide or erase the qualities that make you different—your crazy, curly hair or your superintelligence or your outspoken mom or your high-pitched laugh or your family's financial situation or *whatever*—why not celebrate the awesomely unique ways your garden is different than everyone else's?

The next time you feel that uncomfortable sensation of wanting to erase all your unique qualities, take a moment to stop and think, "I'm going to celebrate who I am instead of fighting it." Remember your imaginary garden and picture your differences as a superspecial and rare flower—something that almost no one else in the entire world has in their garden. Sometimes, this is easier said than actualized. When you actualize a thought, you make it into something you truly believe. Remembering to appreciate your differences over and over again will help you actualize this positive, self-esteem boosting way of thinking.

Another way you can learn to actualize this thought is to celebrate all the ways your family members or friends are unique, too. Remember that everyone yearns to fit in, so the next time you think a friend might be struggling with feeling different, tell them how much you appreciate them for it. Different is beautiful!

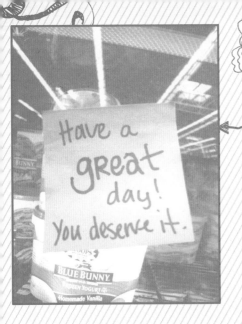

Throughout elementary school and into my middle school years, I definitely wasn't toward the top of the cool-kid food chain. I was just a little more shy, a bit more chubby, and a smidge more awkward than a lot of kids my age. I've always been pretty independent and self-motivated, so during those years, I never thought of myself as being bullied. Looking back, I can see how some of the things kids said, but more so how they treated me, played a part in making me who I am . . . for the better.

I'm now a junior in high school and am pretty content with where I am. I get along with friends from one end of the social spectrum to the other and am involved enough to keep me busy all the time. It's actually pretty neat to stand on one side of the issue, the side of contentment and self-esteem, and be able to reach out and help those who are searching for that same thing. Whether it's leaving an Operation Beautiful note or saying hi to a stranger, I know that the little things mean the most. I can sympathize with that because I've been there.

I wouldn't call myself popular now because that has picked up a negative demeanor over the years. True popularity is a whole lot more about your personality and the ways that you influence others, versus the brand of clothing you wear or the lunch table you sit at.

Meagan, Wisconsin

r u called weird?
Then you are ♡
UNIQUE! ♡
u r Precious ♡
(beautiful heart)

www.
operationbeautiful.
com

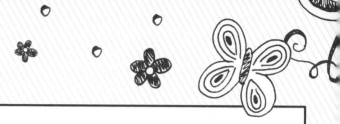

My mom is truly an unsung hero. She has lupus, fibromyalgia, diabetes, asthma, and so many more serious illnesses. The amazing thing about my mom is that she has never stopped going. She is such a strong person. She does almost everything that a regular mother does and can do this only because she pushes herself daily. One of the first effects of lupus was that her hair started falling out. She wore a wig for a little bit, but she stopped because she didn't like it and it itched. Her hair started growing back, but it wasn't full. She does miss her hair at times, and my father has offered to her to get different treatments and operations. My mom says no because that money can be used for other things.

At one time, I had very long hair, and my mom would do my hair for me all the time. I felt that I looked too young with long hair, and I decided to cut it a little shorter than shoulder length. I loved it, but I could tell that my mom did not. Now, I have decided that I will let my hair grow out just for her. I know my mom will read this one day. I just want to say that I'm changing the way I see myself because my mom provided me with such an amazing example. Thank you for showing me how to love myself. Because of this, I can love others—but not more than I love you.

Agatha, Wisconsin

Te necesitamos pues
solo hay una. Eres
unica. Eres tu y para
que sepas eres
Bella asi
Mismito ↓↓↓
Eres una presiosa
gema !

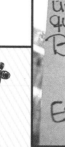

Stepping outside of my comfort zone to accomplish things I never thought I could—that is my favorite thing in the whole world. And when I succeed at that, I feel superconfident. Being able to accomplish what I never thought I could means I have to first forget what the world tells me "I can't do."

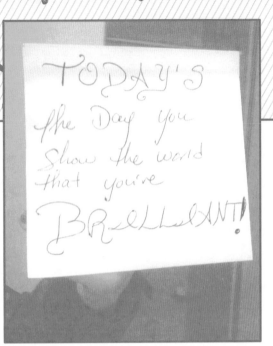

When I was in middle school, the student council president was always an eighth-grade boy. I knew I had a passion for my school and wanted to do the best that I could to improve it. So when I was in seventh grade, I decided to push myself and run for student council president. However, the prospect of running the campaign was intimidating. It was downright scary to have to ask my fellow students to vote for me! That uncomfortable feeling that I got when I had to campaign for votes let me know that I was stepping outside of my comfort zone. Every time I do something that scares me, I get the same feeling. When the campaign ended and the votes came in, all the eighth-grade boys sat next to me in the "candidates row" when they announced: Monika won! The boys couldn't believe it. The eighth-grade class couldn't believe it. I couldn't believe they didn't think I had it in me!

And that's the best part. You DO have it in you! You CAN achieve anything! That power is beautiful! Know that your "inner winner" is just waiting to burst out.

Monika, Colorado

Everyone I know is struggling with something immense, and I'm sure you are, too. For me, illness is the fight. I have a series of silent diseases. Celiac disease, which prohibits me from eating wheat gluten, has to be the most fun (honestly!) of them all. I've fallen in love with food because of it. It has opened my eyes to the world of gluten-free flours. It's incredibly more fun to cook with than wheat flour and tastes wonderful, too! However, having Celiac disease does make me different. I cannot eat everywhere; I have to read the labels of everything I eat or put in my body. I consider it an incredibly small sacrifice. I would rather cut out gluten than return to the days of endless stomachaches and all the other symptoms it brought.

In all the years I've struggled with illness (I'm seventeen now), I've looked fine. When your friends can't particularly see what ails you, it can be difficult. My symptoms have always been quiet—severe exhaustion, brain fog, dizziness, and stomachaches. It was never something clear, like a broken leg or something that hospitalized me. Just because you can't see something, doesn't mean it isn't true. That old adage "don't judge a book by its cover" is an important thing to remember. Through all of this, I've found out who my true friends are, and they've always been the ones who listened when I opened up my heart and in turn, shared their truths with me. Each person I've ever met has beauty within them, not in spite of their trials, but because of how they've dealt with them. Illness has led me to a new passion as well as lifelong friends. It's also made me a more positive, grateful person. It all adds to the unique combination that makes up me, and I wouldn't have it any other way.

Lauren, Alberta, Canada

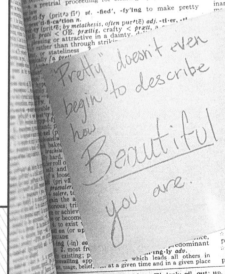

Pretty" doesn't even begin to describe how Beautiful you are.

Self-Esteem Booster: Discover Your Passion

One very cool way that we are all different is that we each have a passion. A passion is a dream about your future or the future of the entire world. Your passion keeps you up late at night as you think about how to make your dreams into reality. Your passion might be about your own personal or professional goals, like wanting to become a doctor or make the soccer team. Your passion can also be about a cause, such as global warming or animal rights.

Passion is so important because it's what gets you out of bed in the morning, excited to tackle a new day! Passion is the thing that keeps you focused on your long-term goals, even when things aren't going as smoothly as you hoped. Passion motivates you and excites you. For these reasons, discovering and honoring your passion is a great way to boost your self-esteem. It's easier to be positive about life when you have that inner fire of passion burning inside you. As a result, you'll be less worried about "fitting in"—you'll be too focused on your passion.

Brittany was thirteen years old when she discovered her passion. "One morning, while getting ready for school and watching the news, I heard a plea from a father of a soldier who was serving in the Middle East. He showed the news reporter a copy of his son's cell phone bill, which was for over $7,000!" Brittany remembers. Sergeant Fletcher had spent thousands calling his family in Massachusetts and was unable to pay the astronomical bill. As a result, the cell phone company had shut off his phone.

A passion is a dream about your future or the future of the entire world.

Brittany turned to her parents and asked a simple question: "Why should this solider be concerned about paying his phone bill when he should really be concerned about keeping himself safe?" Robbie, her twelve-year-old brother, agreed. "We should help him pay the bill," said Robbie. The pair dashed upstairs, grabbed their piggy banks, and dumped the contents out on the kitchen table. Brittany and Robbie's savings totaled $14—not enough, but a start.

"We went to our principal and asked if we could collect money from our classmates as donations to help Sergeant Fletcher pay the bill," Brittany says. "Our friends donated another $7. Our dad took Robbie and me to the South Shore Savings Bank so we could open an account for the donations. The bank manager loved our initiative so much that the bank donated an additional $500!"

Brittany and Robbie organized a car wash, bake sale, and yard sale to help raise even more money. That's when the media started to cover the story. "Robbie and I were interviewed by several local and national television outlets, newspapers, and magazines," Brittany says. People watching or reading about Brittany and Robbie were inspired by their passion, and donations began to pour in. That's when the cell phone company heard about Brittany and Robbie and decided to erase Sergeant Fletcher's bill.

"Why should this solider be concerned about paying his phone bill when he should really be concerned about keeping himself safe?"

By this time, Brittany and Robbie had realized the issue was much bigger than Sergeant Fletcher's $7,000 bill—all the American soldiers overseas needed a way to call home! "We wanted to help make sure that our troops would never have to worry about affording to make a phone call to their loved ones," she says proudly. "That's when Cell Phones for Soldiers was born."

People all over the country mailed Brittany and Robbie donations and old cell phones, which the siblings were hoping to fill with prepaid minutes and mail to the Middle East. "Almost immediately, we received a call from the Pentagon. The army said that we couldn't send cell phones over because it was a security risk," says Brittany. "I was so nervous when I heard that!" Plus, Brittany and Robbie's house was filled with old phones—what were they going to do with them?

The pair refused to let this obstacle derail their plans; they studied the situation carefully and tried to come up with a creative solution. "I knew about recycling companies that would give points to schools so that teachers could buy equipment for their classrooms," says Brittany. "I contacted several and asked if they would consider recycling the phones for cash. We settled on one company, who is still our recycling partner." Cell Phones for Soldiers uses the cash from recycled cell phones to buy prepaid calling cards, which Brittany and Robbie then send overseas to soldiers so they can call home for free.

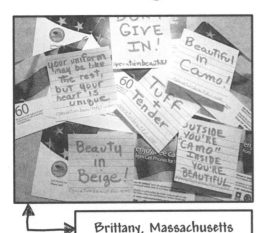

Brittany, Massachusetts

Amazingly, the nonprofit Brittany and Robbie created out of their home has grown into a multimillion dollar nonprofit organization. "Cell Phones for Soldiers has recycled over seven million phones and has sent one and a half million minutes of talk time to troops serving on military bases and recuperating in hospitals throughout the world," reports Brittany. And all it took was one small hope that they could help someone in need.

Do you know your passion? Don't feel bad if the answer is no! Lots of people, including adults, aren't sure what passion lies deep within their hearts. They might not feel drawn to any cause or career in particular, or they might like—but don't *love*—a lot of different things. If you're searching for your passion, don't worry—you can find it!

- **Don't Doubt Yourself:** Get rid of all the "would've" and "should've" thoughts that are racing through your head. Often we ignore the inner voice that tells us about our passions because we're afraid of what other people will think. Or maybe we think other people will think our idea is crazy or far-fetched! Listen to your heart—what do you really get excited about? Don't judge your desires; just let them come to you!
- **Your Passion Might Be Hiding at School:** Often, people are drawn to certain subjects in school because they relate to their passion. If you love English class, your passion might have to do with reading, writing, or teaching. If you love biology, maybe your passion lies in the medical field, research, or environmental sciences. How you prefer to do work might also offer clues to your passion; for example, do you like to work in groups? Do you like to give speeches or debates?
- **If You Would Do It for Free, It Might be Your Passion:** Chores are never fun, but most kids will do them with a smile if their parents give them an allowance. Lots of adults feel that way about their jobs; they don't really enjoy what they do, but they'll do it because they get paid! Is there anything in your life that others would consider work, but you'd be happy to do it for free? For example, maybe you love volunteering with the younger kids at Sunday school, really enjoy walking your neighbor's dog, or had so much fun planting trees on Earth Day. If so, you might be passionate about teaching, animals, or the environment!

- **Skills Can Be Passions:** Everyone is good at different things. Some people are born great listeners; this is a wonderful skill that might reveal a passion for volunteering at a retirement home. Or maybe you're good at math and could use your skills to help raise money for a charity.
- **Passions Can Change:** A passion isn't necessarily for life. Some things might interest you one year, and something new will tickle your fancy the next! Don't get too worried if your interests or passions change; that's all just part of growing up and maturing. Keep your mind open to new possibilities!
- **The Great Unknown Passion:** If you've carefully thought about all areas of your life but are still stumped, your passion might truly be undiscovered. This isn't a bad thing—it's actually pretty exciting, if you think about it. The options are limitless! Try some new extracurricular activities or volunteer on the weekends. Something you've never even heard of before might peak your interest. You could even do a whole year of volunteering at a new place each month. After twelve months, you will have twelve totally unique experiences that just might clue you into your passion.

✵ Do It Now! ✵ Volunteer to Discover Your Passion

Check out these online resources to find a volunteering opportunity that is perfect for you!

1. Kids Care Clubs—kidscare.org
2. Volunteer Match—volunteermatch.org
3. Idealist—idealist.org
4. Take Pride in America—takepride.gov
5. Habitat for Humanity—habitat.org
6. Keep America Beautiful—kab.org
7. Do Something—dosomething.org
8. Service Nation—servicenation.org

One of the best ways to boost your own self-esteem is to volunteer to help other people, animals, or the planet. Volunteering with others will boost your confidence, remind you of your blessings, refocus your attention on inner beauty, and help you realize how amazing *you* can be! No matter what your interests, there is a volunteering opportunity that aligns perfectly with your passions.

One of the best ways to boost your own self-esteem is to volunteer to help other people, animals, or the planet.

Does your passion call you to volunteer with animals? Do you feel strongly about saving the planet, stopping the spread of diseases like AIDS, halting discrimination or bullying, helping our troops, increasing awareness about poverty, assisting victims of domestic violence, or aiding people following a natural disaster? How can you change your community? How can you change the *world*? Dream big!

Dreaming big is very important, but you should also be realistic so your volunteering dreams are achievable. Identifying your passion is the first step; the second piece of your puzzle is developing an *action plan*. If you want to simply volunteer with an organization that is already in place, your action plan might be very simple, such as "I want to save the planet, so I'm going to volunteer on a community clean-up day." However, if you want to create a charity from the ground up like Brittany did, your action plan will be more complex.

Fast Fact: Good for Them, Good for You!

Studies show that people who are involved in community service are more satisfied with life, have higher self-esteem, possess a sense of purpose, and are in better physical and mental health than people who don't.

Word Up) Action Plan

An action plan describes what you want, the steps required to reach your goal, and solutions to possible obstacles. You can create an action plan for any aspect of your life—whether it's reaching a goal at school, organizing a community service project, or adopting healthier habits.

You should write your action plan down on paper or on the computer. Don't just keep your action plan in your head! Writing down our goals makes them seem more real, and as a result, we're more likely to stick to our plan. The first part of your action plan is your mission statement. A **mission statement** describes your passion and your goals. An example of a mission statement is: "I want to create a club at school that is dedicated to collecting warm winter clothes for homeless people in my community. I want to raise awareness about homelessness and remind homeless people that the rest of the community cares about them."

> Writing down our goals makes them seem more real, and as a result, we're more likely to stick to our plan.

Next, carefully think about all the steps necessary to reach your goal. You might want to brainstorm—which is when you share ideas and listen to suggestions—with a family member or friend, especially if that person might have specialized knowledge about your topic. Establish target dates for reaching your smaller goals to help you stay on track. For example, "The first step is talking to my principal about the clothing drive by the end of next week." Try to also think of potential problems or obstacles that you might encounter and come up with solutions in advance.

A mission statement describes your passion and your goals.

"There were definitely people who doubted Cell Phones for Soldiers," says Brittany. "One of the biggest obstacles was convincing people that Robbie and I were sincere about our program." The pair overcame this obstacle by remaining true to the core mission of Cell Phones for Soldiers, which was to help soldiers call home, and not get distracted by all the media attention. "I've also had to learn to manage my time so I don't get overwhelmed or frustrated," says Brittany, who is now a college sophomore and majoring in business and marketing.

"My advice to tweens or teens who are hoping to start their own charity would be to be prepared for hard work and don't get discouraged when things are not going the way you had hoped," she reflects. "It does get easier once everything is established, but starting out is very challenging. Seek out adults and mentors who can assist you with any questions you may have, and don't be afraid to ask for help from major corporations. Many companies are looking for ways to help in their communities and will be more than happy to assist!" To learn more about Brittany's mission, visit Cell Phones for Soldiers on the web at cellphonesforsoldiers.com.

> "One of the biggest obstacles was convincing people that Robbie and I were sincere about our program."

The thing that I love most about me is my personality! I am very peppy and hopelessly optimistic about everything. To most of my friends at times it can get really annoying, since they don't understand how I can have such a positive outlook on things that would make them upset. I always think, "What's the point in getting upset? It won't get me anywhere and who likes feeling mad?" It's not a great way to go and live, so I just don't do it!

Kennedy, Ontario, Canada

I volunteer at a domestic violence shelter with my church for the homeless and less fortunate and for an eating disorder center as a mentor, group leader, and office assistant. Volunteering makes my heart smile. There is no greater feeling than knowing you made someone's day and possibly their entire year—all by taking the time out of our busy schedules and doing good for others. When I feel like my life is too dark or too difficult to keep going, I reach out and help someone. There are people who have had a very tough life and yet they have insurmountable strength and determination. Volunteering is a two-way street; when I do it I am both giving and receiving. Those who I volunteer for give me hope, strengthen my faith, open my eyes, put more love into my heart, and make me very grateful.

Katherine, California

I'm passionate about helping other people. I want to help other people by continuing to post notes for Operation Beautiful so others know that they're beautiful just as they are. But I also want to spread the word about suicide awareness and prevention. I've wanted to do this ever since I learned about an organization called To Write Love On Her Arms, and I've joined numerous support groups on Facebook that share the same vision as TWLOHA. I've made so many friends through the groups, and I love each and every one of them. I want to help more people by telling them that they are not alone, and rescue is possible.

Mackenzie, Indiana

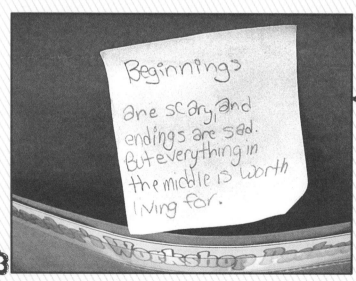

Debra, New York

Your Beautiful Body: Focused on Health, Not Image

While the media tries to convince you that looking "perfect" is beautiful, the truth is that health is stunning—and health comes in many different shapes, sizes, and colors. Respecting and taking care of our bodies is a truly beautiful thing. This section explores how you can become the healthiest—and happiest—version of your perfectly amazing self.

A Healthy Goal

Our society places too much importance on what we look like. We hear this message from friends and family members who might not realize what they're saying (like Fat Talk and other types of negative self-talk); we also hear this message from the media in magazines and on television shows. In very subtle ways, our society says that, for girls and women, all that matters is looking perfect and fitting into the Thin Ideal. This negative messaging impacts us in two ways. First, it hurts us *physically* by convincing us that we need to diet, overexercise, or use lots of beauty products to look "perfect." Second, it hurts us *emotionally* by chipping away at our sense of self-esteem.

Not only do these negative messages have a huge impact on our well-being, but the messages are just flat-out wrong! The truth is that being healthy is the most important thing. Healthy is about being strong (mentally and physically) and happy. It's about respecting your body because it's the only one you've got!

It's time we change things. And *you* have the power to do this! Instead of focusing on looking perfect, let's focus on being healthy.

While our society wants you to think that looking good equals being healthy, Operation Beautiful knows that health is about much more. Health involves your body *and* mind. Just like being healthy isn't about being a particular size, health isn't only about exercising and eating vegetables! Health is truly tied to your sense of self-worth—that's why the section entitled A Beautiful Mind comes before A Beautiful Body in this book! Being mentally healthy involves positive self-talk, volunteering or helping other people, accepting your differences, being kind and not bullying, and taking other proactive steps to build your self-esteem.

Physical health is about much more than your weight. (The relationship between health and weight is discussed in the next chapter.) Your body is a wonderful and crazily complicated machine! Have you ever thought of your body as a machine? Your body is like the world's most intelligent computer. Isn't it amazing to consider all that your body can do? Your body runs all day and all night long—breathing, walking, pumping blood, laughing, seeing, speaking, understanding, digesting—and most of us never take the time to appreciate the wonder and complexity of these processes! Physical health is about how well our bodies can do all the things it's designed for. Physical health is impacted by many factors, like drinking enough water, getting adequate sleep, the genetic predispositions your parents handed down to you, getting the right amount of nutritious foods, and exercising or playing sports regularly. Weight is just one factor of physical health.

For a variety of reasons, most people don't strive to be mentally and physically healthy; they just want to "look good." But there's a major problem with focusing solely on appearance: When our only goal is to "look good," we often engage in unhealthy and very dangerous habits, like negative self-talk, not eating enough food or eating the wrong types of foods, and exercising too much or not exercising at all! These unhealthy habits can cause a ton of problems, like having trouble concentrating at school, getting sick easily, or even weakening your bones to the point where they're more likely to break!

People who focus on their appearance instead of health tend to waver between two extremes: total commitment and totally slacking off. Have you ever heard an adult in your life talk about going on a new fad diet that sounds really strict, like not eating bread or never eating dessert? This is called a "crash diet" and is a perfect example of an unhealthy and extreme behavior that people engage in when trying to "look good." Bet they didn't stay on that diet for very long!

✹ Do It Now! ✹ Health 411

Most adults would say that healthy people eat well, get enough sleep, exercise regularly, and drink lots of water. While this is certainly true, it's also pretty vague!

⚡ Do It Now! ⚡ Health 411 (cont)

How much sleep is "enough sleep" for a girl your age, for example? What if you toss and turn all night long? Why are vegetables so important? Can you drink *too much* water? Does soda count as water? And do you *really* need to floss every day?

If you want to learn more about being healthy, check out these websites:

- Kids Health at kidshealth.org
- BAM! Body and Mind at bam.gov
- Health Information for Girls at girlshealth.gov

Help!: "Whenever my friends complain about their looks, I tell them to stop it and that they are truly beautiful. However, I cannot apply this kind of thinking to myself!"

Do you say or think things about yourself that you would never, ever say to a friend? If so, you might be lacking some self-compassion. Self-compassion means "going easy" on yourself when you come across things you may not like about yourself or don't reach a goal.

The next time you start to beat yourself up for something, remember the acronym PEDAL, which stands for **P**ositive thinking, **E**veryone experiences, **D**rama free, **A**cceptance, and **L**ove. Let's apply the PEDAL solution to the real-life problem above: You accept that your friends are beautiful because of their internal qualities, but you cannot believe you are beautiful, too.

- **P**ositive thinking: When you start to have these thoughts, replace them with a positive and realistic thought, such as, "Even though I might doubt myself, I know I am beautiful, too, because I am just as loving and kind as my friends."
- **E**veryone experiences: You can develop self-compassion by reminding yourself that everyone suffers from feelings of not being good enough. You're not alone in fighting this battle!
- **D**rama free: Sometimes, we make situations more dramatic than necessary. If you feel yourself getting overly emotional about a situation, remember that you're in control and can choose to react in a more positive, stress-free way.
- **A**cceptance: Do you place unfair demands on yourself, like having to be "perfect"? We accept others, flaws and all. Remember that you can accept yourself, too!
- **L**ove: Even when you aren't thinking negatively, tell yourself loving things! Remind yourself constantly—not just when you already feel bad—how truly amazing you are. Remember, you're your own best friend!

In contrast, when you focus on being healthy, you're in it for the long haul! There's no need to be extreme in your behaviors because you're all about being healthy for *the rest of your life*! You focus on eating nutritious foods because it helps your body— the amazing machine—run smoothly and efficiently. You get off the couch and play outside instead of watching television because it's good for your muscles, reduces stress, and is fun! You minimize negative self-talk and encourage positivity. You put down your awesome new book, turn off the light, and go to bed early because you can think so much more clearly at school the next day.

The other advantage to focusing on being healthy is it doesn't require that you be "perfect" all the time. The Healthy Ideal is about being balanced in your food choices and physical activity. A good word to remember is *moderation*, which means you don't do anything too much or too little.

Let's pretend that being healthy is like riding a bicycle. When you make healthy choices, you're pedaling quickly and efficiently on the bike, so you speed along. When you make unhealthy choices, it's like your feet stop moving for a moment. If your feet stop pedaling for a little bit, the bike still coasts forward, right? But if you make too many unhealthy choices and stop pedaling for a long, long time, the bike slows down. You get slower and slower until you eventually crash! When you live a healthy lifestyle, you choose healthy options more than you choose unhealthy options. Enjoying desserts or fried food every now and then is fine as long as you enjoy these foods in moderation and make healthy choices more often than not. No one wants to crash their bike, right?!

Being healthy isn't about being strict or never having fun—it's all about making small choices that add up over time and contribute to a healthier, happier you!

The other advantage to focusing on being healthy is it doesn't require that you be "perfect" all the time.

And guess what? Focusing on health over appearance actually has a very surprising benefit. Have you ever noticed that if you don't sleep well for a few days in a row, you get dark circles underneath your eyes? Or if you don't drink enough water during the summer, your skin starts to look all dry and flaky? When you don't take care of your body, it shows all over your face! By focusing on being healthy, your skin will be clearer, your hair will be shinier, and your eyes will be brighter. And that's a beautiful thing!

Journal It: My Beautiful and Healthy Body!

Most of us spend too much time criticizing our appearance. Let's focus on the positive—and on all the cool stuff our body allows us to do! Make a list of everything you like about your body and why in your journal. Try to focus on the things your body allows you to do, like dancing or singing.

Here's an example: I love my legs because they can kick a soccer ball very far!

Fast Fact: Eat to Become Smarter!

Did you know that eating healthy foods can actually make you smarter? Foods such as salmon, walnuts, and kiwi contain healthy components called Omega-3 fatty acids, which help to build connections in your brain as you learn new information. In one study, kids who consumed Omega-3s and other important nutrients found in fruits and vegetables earned high scores on verbal and memory tests!

On the other hand, there have been several scientific studies that illustrate eating junk food or fast food actually decreases your brain power, making it harder to learn new information.

Bet you'll never look at broccoli the same way again!

For as long as I can remember, I have been a competitive figure skater. When I skated, I absolutely loved it. I felt strong and beautiful. I thought I would do it for the rest of my life. This year I decided to stop because I couldn't find the love that I have always had for the sport. What I really wanted to try next was singing and taking acting lessons. I took a class with kids I didn't know in another city and really loved it. However, as much as I loved performing, I didn't like being out of shape, so I started to run, and I felt the best I had in a long time, physically and emotionally. But after eight months and a couple injuries, my coach told me to stop. I am only twelve, and I had to let my body grow some more because running was hard on my joints and muscles.

Not being active made me feel terrible because I got out of shape. For the first time ever, I hated my body. So I've decided to try something new. I have joined a precompetitive swim team. With the way I feel about my body lately, I don't really want to be in a bathing suit. But the need to feel healthy and great again has won over feeling unattractive.

What I know is that taking risks is for the best. No matter what I do and try, I know that with hard work I can do well. I also have learned that I love doing lots of different things, and that is a better fit for me than just being great at one thing.

Kennedy, Ontario, Canada

FORGET THIN...
WORK ON HEALTHY...
YOU ARE MORE BEAUTIFUL
HEALTHY THAN THIN!

www.operationbeautiful.com

When I was growing up, I struggled with wanting to fit in, just like most teens do. What people thought of me was very important to me and had a strong influence on how I tried to live my life. Don't get me wrong—I was happy, I was loved by my family, and my friends and I had great, fun times together. Looking back at those years, I now realize that what guided me in many of my decisions was the desire to fit in and be liked by others. I never thought about whether I liked myself! I now know that it's okay to live your life in a way that makes you happy.

I have struggled with weight all of my life. I've been on more diets than I care to remember. I've always focused on trying to look good, to be thin, or to wear smaller sizes. It has taken me fifty years to learn that being thin is not what is important. Being healthy is what makes us all beautiful, regardless of our size. If we strive to be healthy, beauty automatically follows. My goal at this age is to forget the diets, to focus on becoming more physically active, and to love myself for who I am and for the positive impact I have on those around me. Because, you see, I am beautiful—and I always have been!

Cris, Virginia

I was the daughter of a small-town minister and a well-known teacher. I was a musician and a varsity athlete. I had amazing friends. I had a fantastic support system. But I wasn't . . . popular. I wasn't heavy, but I wasn't skinny. I wasn't ugly, but I wasn't pretty. I wasn't weird, but I wasn't cool. I just . . . was. The popular crowd didn't shun me, but they didn't exactly welcome me with open arms. I used to see their confidence and happiness and wish I could be a part of it—just for one moment. I was a "Someday Dreamer." I would close my eyes and imagine myself someday wearing the perfect clothes and looking beautiful like the other girls did. I wished someday I could walk down the hallways at school hand in hand with my boyfriend and laughing with my friends. But that just wasn't who I was. Maybe it would be someday, but not then.

At some point, I found myself. I learned how to embrace the things that I am passionate about and dive into them with confidence and good faith. I only wish that I hadn't let the popular crowd get to me back then. I wish I had been confident in who I was and not who I wanted to be. I wish I had been okay with me.

My hope for any tweens or teens struggling to find their identity is that they look in the mirror and see someone looking back who is beautiful, confident, and worthy of feeling fabulous. My prayer is that they will find and pursue their passion. Don't wait ten years to find happiness. My advice for the "Someday Dreamers" is this: Make "someday" . . . today.

Sarah, Connecticut

"Why compare yourself with others? No one in the entire world can do a better job of being you than you." —unknown.

www.operationbeautiful.com

Sienna, Ohio

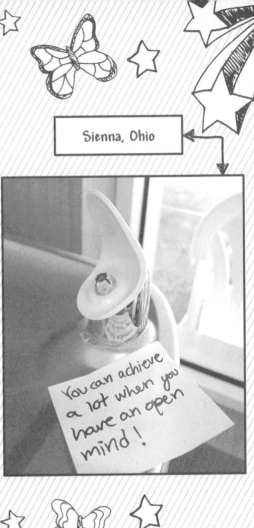

You can achieve a lot when you have an open mind!

When I was thirteen years old, a boy in my class called me "fat" and I started seeing myself in this negative way. I became so obsessed with how I looked that I developed an eating disorder. I based my happiness on the number on the scale, but I was never satisfied. I was lucky that people close to me noticed my problem and got me help.

Looking back, I wish I would have been able to think differently about myself. Beauty is not based on someone else's perception of you; it is based on your own perception of yourself. I was beautiful then and I am beautiful now—and it is about time we all start to realize that we are all beautiful and that we all deserve to feel this way.

Gillian, Manitoba, Canada

Health and Weight

Can you look at someone and tell if they are healthy? Well, you know the old saying—don't judge a book by its cover! Just because a girl is thin doesn't mean she's healthy on the inside . . . mentally or physically. And being a little overweight doesn't automatically mean you're physically unhealthy, either.

Imagine a girl who falls within the "healthy weight" range, but she hates sports, smokes cigarettes, skips meals, and eats a big candy bar every day. Now, imagine another girl who is naturally curvier and has the same "big-boned" structure as her mom. This girl plays softball for her school, eats lots of vegetables and fruits, and takes her dogs for walks when she needs to de-stress. Despite the fact that the second girl has a higher weight, she is probably a much healthier person than the first girl!

The Healthy Ideal says that health can come in a variety of shapes and sizes because we all have different body types. Our body type is determined by many factors, including our parents' body types.

 Journal It: My Body Type

Healthy bodies come in different weights, heights, and shapes; some girls naturally have larger hips while others have larger shoulders. Some girls' bodies are straight up and down, like a ruler! Your body type might even change during your teenage years as you go through puberty.

What's your shape?

Apple: Apple girls have wider shoulders, busts, and waists than hips and legs.

Journal It: My Body Type (cont)

Banana: Banana girls don't have many curves or a big difference between their upper and lower bodies.

Pear: Pear girls have wider hips and legs than shoulders and bust.

Hourglass: Hourglass girls have a waist that tucks in, and their bust is the same size as their hips.

If you don't see a shape that sounds like your body type in the list above, you can make one up. Maybe you feel like a pear on top and an hourglass on the bottom—your unique shape can be "pearglass" or "banapple"!

Body shapes are one of the primary reasons why it doesn't make sense to compare your body to other people, especially if you don't have the same shape! An apple can't jump onto a banana tree, paint itself yellow, and pretend to be a banana. It wouldn't fool anyone!

All body shapes are beautiful and attractive in their own ways; however, all shapes are challenging to dress in their own ways. If you're an apple, you might struggle finding tops that fit; if you're a banana, the butt of jeans might always be too big on you. Search the Internet for the keywords "How to dress for my body type" to discover easy tips on how to select outfits that are most flattering for your awesome natural shape.

Answer the following questions in your journal. If you have a picture of yourself rockin' your favorite outfit, paste it into your journal, too!

What's my body type?

What do I like about my body type?

What's my favorite outfit to wear and how does it flatter my body shape?

Although weight is not the end all be all, it *does* matter when it comes to your health. Doctors are concerned about your weight because too little or too much extra body fat, regardless of your natural body shape, can be harmful to your health. Being dangerously overweight is much more common than being dangerously underweight, although both problems are serious. One out of three kids and teens between the ages of two and nineteen is overweight or obese. (Two out of every three adults are overweight or obese.)

Extra body fat means that your body's organs, like your lungs and heart, have to work especially hard to function properly, which can make it hard to walk up the stairs, run during recess, or even sleep soundly at night. Being overweight can also lead to problems like diabetes and acid reflux, plus loads of other serious health complications down the road.

Fast Fact: Get Moving to Stay Healthy!

A scale cannot tell you how healthy you are—you really can't judge health by appearance! Researchers have identified a condition known as TOFI—"Thin Outside, Fat Inside." People who are TOFIs appear to be a healthy weight but have excess levels of body fat around their important internal organs. You can't see this extra fat, but it can cause many of the same health issues as being overweight. According to data, TOFI is most common in people who don't exercise regularly. Everyone—regardless of their natural body shape— needs exercise to keep in tip-top shape, so turn off the television, get off the couch, and *move*! Play your favorite sport, walk your dog, or dance to your favorite song in your living room.

Doctors have created a scientific way to determine if someone's weight falls within a healthy range. Doctors use a tool called the Body Mass Index (BMI) calculation, which compares your height to your weight while accounting for your age and gender. Your BMI calculation lets the doctor know if your weight falls into the underweight, healthy weight, overweight, or obese (which means very overweight) ranges. Each category includes a range of weights to account for the fact that a healthy girl who is five feet tall could be pear-shaped and therefore weigh more naturally than a healthy friend who is also five feet tall but banana-shaped.

People become overweight for several reasons. First, they might eat or drink more calories (which is a measurement of how much energy is in food) than their body can use. As a result, their body stores the extra calories as fat. Over time, the more extra food a person eats, the more fat they gain. Secondly, a person might become overweight because they spend too much time sitting in front of computers or the television instead of playing sports, riding bikes, exploring the neighborhood on foot, or exercising in another way. When we move our bodies, we use calories to fuel ourselves. By sitting around all the time, we aren't transforming any of the food we're eating into fuel to run our bodies, so our bodies store it as fat. A lot of people in America overeat *and* don't get any exercise, which is a double whammy.

When we move our bodies, we use calories to fuel ourselves.

In fact, if you look around at our society, there are a lot of reasons why more and more people are dangerously overweight. Fast-food restaurants are everywhere—and the food is supercheap! There are tons of cool inventions—like television, Internet, and cell phones—that encourage people to sit around and stare at a screen instead of moving their bodies. Most cities are designed in a way that discourages walking and forces people to drive everywhere. And kids and adults are pressured to spend a lot of time at school or work; some people are so overscheduled that they might feel like there isn't time to play or exercise. These reasons are called environmental factors and greatly contribute to the reason our country is more overweight than ever.

A lot of people in America overeat and don't get any exercise, which is a double whammy.

Some people are overweight because of health problems that they can't control. The body naturally secretes hormones that regulate its functions, like blood production or food digestion. Too little or too much of certain hormones can cause weight issues. Weight problems can also be caused by food allergies. If you feel like you're doing all the right things—eating healthy and moving your body—but are still overweight, talk to your doctor about your situation. For most people, however, healthy habits can make a big difference in helping them reach a healthy weight.

The issue of weight and health has so many layers, doesn't it? So what's a girl to do if she is overweight and her doctors say it's bad for her health?

Word Up)Happy Weight

Your Happy Weight is a healthy weight that you reach through healthy eating and fun exercise. It's the weight that your body naturally maintains when you eat healthy foods and enjoy treats in moderation. Your Happy Weight might not be the weight that the Thin Ideal says you "should weigh"—but you already know that the Thin Ideal promotes being at an unhealthily low weight! You can find your Happy Weight by following good habits that are in line with the Healthy Ideal and embracing your natural body shape. Numbers on a scale don't tell the whole story about health. And a scale certainly cannot tell you how amazing you are—scales measure weight, not worth!

In order to find your Happy Weight, all girls need to take a careful look at their own habits, their family's and friends' habits, environmental factors that might impact their healthy lifestyle, and their personal and family's medical history. Your doctor can determine if medical issues are contributing to your unhealthy weight; if so, your doctor can provide you with the right treatment for better health.

Regardless of your weight, we can all work to be healthier!

The simple truth is that most people struggle with unhealthy weight due to lifestyle choices and environmental factors. Fortunately, your lifestyle choices and how you react to environmental factors are entirely within your control. Regardless of your weight, we can all work to be healthier! The next chapter discusses how you can develop healthier eating and exercise habits, and it also provides tips for being healthy in a world that promotes unhealthy behaviors. Operation Beautiful doesn't want you to feel restricted or stressed out in any way while you try to reach your Healthy Ideal and Happy Weight—being healthy can be fun and exciting!

Feeling healthy, strong, confident... THAT is true beauty.

www.operationbeautiful.com

Liz, Ohio

I think being healthy means truly listening to your body. I could never have gotten to where I'm at with the love for my body if I hadn't listened to it. When my body tells me it's craving a cookie, I eat it in a healthy amount. When it wants to be active, I do something I love like bike riding with my family. Just listen to yourself and obey your body in a healthy way!

Sarah, Georgia

I don't like how my body isn't "model thin." These negative ideas about my body came from one of my old friends that told me I was fat. I try not to compare my body to other people, but it's hard not to do so. I hear my friends talk badly about their bodies all the time. Half of the time, they are just moaning about their natural body type! I always tell them, "You are beautiful, no matter what. God never makes mistakes, and he made you."

Emma, Australia

I was in seventh grade, and the boys in my class nicknamed me Buffalo Butt. Those boys taunted me during the one-mile fitness test in gym class. "Hey, Buffalo Butt, you are running really slow!" Those boys slammed my locker shut while I put away my books. "Hey, Buffalo Butt, you aren't very smart!" Those boys yelled across the dining hall while I quietly ate my lunch. "Hey, Buffalo Butt. You are fat!" Those boys stole my confidence.

In middle school, I tried everything to lose weight. I cut out fitness tips from beauty magazines and even ordered a weight loss kit from the back of a teen magazine. When it arrived in the mail, my dad intercepted the package. I lied and told him that I didn't know why my name was on the box and that it must have been a mistake. I turned to food to make myself feel better, but I was miserable inside. I desperately wanted a boy to ask me out and wanted to fit into the trendy baby T-shirts that were so popular.

While it has taken me countless years and struggles with eating and an unhealthy lifestyle, something clicked in my late twenties while on a casual run after work. I am in control of my happiness. Once I realized that I am a smart, kind, sensitive, and genuine woman, self-confidence naturally crept back into my life. I started to learn, and believe, that staying true to me and doing what makes me happy are qualities more beautiful than any physical feature. I still think about my junior high nickname every once in a while, but instead of crying, I laugh because those boys are not a part of my life anymore. I am in control. And you know what? I finally snagged a man of my own who loves me most when I'm not wearing any makeup.

Michelle, Oregon

"Always be a first rate version of yourself, not a second rate version of someone else."
~Judy Garland

www.operationbeautiful.com

Inner beauty is the only beauty that counts!! You're beautiful in every way!

www.operationbeautiful.com

What you see is ONLY part of your Beauty..

www.operati...bea...

Elizabeth, Utah

I'm thirteen years old. When I get teased about my weight, it's hard to turn the other cheek. It's hard because it makes you feel bad about yourself and like you're this little person under a microscope. When you're teased by your friends, it's always difficult to keep your mouth closed and just try to laugh it off.

When I look at pretty, skinny girls, I always get a little jealous, thinking to myself, "What if you were like that? You could get boys all the time!" or "You wouldn't have to get all those raggedy clothes that are not as pretty as the skinny girls wear." But when I look at myself in the mirror, I also see a pretty, amazing, talented thirteen-year-old that has the power and brains to one day become an ultrasonographer, my dream job. I know that looks aren't everything, even if sometimes it feels like they are.

Katie, North Carolina

As a sixteen-year-old high school student, I see low self-esteem every day. I have friends who will complain about the many things they see wrong with themselves. I also have had days when all I can see is the bad in myself. After realizing how much self-destructive talk was occurring just in my own group of friends, I knew that it must be everywhere. I began to challenge myself to find the most beautiful feature about a person. It was easier than I thought it would be, and when I began to look for beautiful things in other people, it made it a lot easier to see the beauty within myself.

But as I noticed all of these beautiful things, I wanted to tell the person what I thought, but I am fairly quiet and timid. Only a few times did I ever have the courage to directly tell someone why they were beautiful. The satisfaction it gave me was enormous, and so I was excited to find Operation Beautiful, a way for me to tell people that they are beautiful. When I'm feeling stressed or sad, I fill up pads of Post-it notes with inspirational phrases, and once I've put them up in my school, I can't help but smile the entire day, knowing that someone will find my notes and feel better.

Lauren, Ontario, Canada

Healthy Fuel

One way to treat your body with the respect that it deserves is to fill it with healthy, natural foods. Many people think they need to go on a "diet" to eat healthy, but the truth is that diets are often unhealthy. There's a better way to eat—and you can still enjoy dessert!

Down with Diets!

Turn on the TV, flip through a magazine, or browse the bookstore—you'll notice that diets are a hot topic, especially if it's after New Year's Eve or close to the summertime. You might have even heard your mom or friends talking about going on a diet. "Lose five pounds a week!" some diets proclaim. "Limit carbs and blast away belly fat!" another promises. At its most simple definition, a "diet" is what a person typically eats and drinks. But in everyday conversation, "diet" usually refers to a short-term, restrictive style of eating that promises to help you lose weight or tone up. When we use the word "diet" in this book, we're referring to this type of diet.

It's easy to spot a diet. Diets promise fast fixes in a short amount of time and clearly label some foods as "good" and others as "bad." Each diet swears that it's the best way to lose weight through a certain trick, such as not eating carbohydrates, eating more protein, not eating white foods, not eating after a certain time of day, or even only eating cabbage soup! Sometimes diets masquerade as a healthy way of eating, but if you look closely, the diet restricts your food intake or banishes desserts. If you're considering a "healthy eating plan" but can't imagine yourself eating that way forever, it's really just a plain old diet.

Fast Fact: Puberty Changes Everything

Did you know your body changes and grows faster during puberty than it will at any other time of your life, not counting infancy? Puberty usually starts between ages eight and thirteen in girls, although it's normal for girls to start earlier or later. Puberty is when your body transitions from being a kid's body to an adult's body, and the whole process is caused by the release of new hormones by your brain. These hormones not only impact your body's growth, but they can also temporarily affect the way you feel emotionally—many girls going through puberty report mood swings or irritability.

Puberty can make you taller (or not), make your breasts grow (or not), and cause you to gain weight in your hips or rear (or not). You'll also get your period (some girls get it sooner than others). Your hair color may change; your underarm, pubic, or leg hair might grow in darker or thicker; and your voice can even become deeper! Puberty looks different for different people.

It's common to feel stressed out about these body changes, especially when you compare your body to your friends'. Some girls might Fat Talk about their new bodies or try to "diet away" their new hips or breasts. However, because your body is going through such drastic changes, it's even more important to fuel it with healthy foods, get enough sleep, drink enough water, and be active. Puberty can be confusing and sometimes even scary, but just remember that changes in your body are normal. If you have any questions, you can always ask your doctor at the next checkup—he or she has heard *everything* before, so don't be embarrassed to ask.

Word Up) Calories

A *calorie* is a measurement of how much energy is in food. In order to run properly, your body needs a certain number of calories every day. If your body is a machine, imagine that calories are like gas!

Different people have different calorie needs because of their gender, body shape, and activity level; daily needs for growing tweens and teens can vary from fifteen hundred to three thousand calories a day—in general, older and more active boys need more calories than younger and less active girls. Over time, if you regularly eat more calories than you need, your body stores the calories as body fat. All calories are not the same—some foods provide more important nutrients calorie by calorie than others. For example, a candy bar and a bowl of whole grain cereal with milk and a banana might have the same calories, but the cereal is much healthier because it provides you with vitamins, minerals, carbohydrates, protein, and fiber, while the candy bar provides only sugar and fat!

Some diets heavily focus on counting calories; however, this practice can become a little obsessive and over the top. After all, it's nearly impossible to know *exactly* how many calories you need or *exactly* how many calories are in everything you eat! Additionally, putting the focus on calories distracts you from the real goal: eating quality, nutritious foods that fill you up and make you feel good! So, instead of counting calories, check out a food's nutrition facts to ensure you're eating nutritious foods (there are more details about nutrition facts later in this chapter!).

Diets are false promises. Although you might lose weight at first, diets simply do not work in the long-term. People quickly gain back whatever weight they lost on a diet because they eventually return to their normal style of eating. In fact, studies show that 30 to 60 percent of dieters regain *more weight* than they lost on their diets!

Why do diets fail?
- Diets don't teach healthy habits, preach moderation (which means you don't eat too little or too much of any food), or focus on long-term happiness. Diets are restrictive (which means you don't have a lot of freedom with your food choices) and difficult to maintain for long periods of time.
- Diets label some foods as "good" and others as "bad." The truth is that all foods can be enjoyed in a healthy manner; it's just important to eat less-healthy foods in moderation.
- Dieting makes you feel superhungry. When you restrict your calorie level to a dangerously low level, the diet backfires. You become sick to your stomach, light-headed, and miserable. When you're hungry, it's hard to make healthy food choices.
- Diets increase cravings. When you believe certain foods are off-limits, you tend to want them even more!
- Diets promote an "all-or-nothing" attitude about eating. You might stay on the diet for a day or two and then feel defeated if you have a dessert after dinner. Dieters usually toss in the towel and end up eating more unhealthy stuff than ever before.
- Since diets are not successful in the long-term, some people spend their whole lives hopping from one diet to the next, searching for a permanent fix. This is dangerous because constant changes in your weight put a big strain on your body.

One huge problem with diets is that they mess up your ability to listen to physical hunger cues (like a rumbling stomach), which is your body's way of telling you that it needs more fuel! If you're on a diet, you only eat when you're "supposed to" and might avoid snacks when you're hungry. If a diet backfires, you might end up eating lots of food, way past the point of being full. Diets can hurt your natural ability to tell if you're hungry or full. This impact of dieting can last long after the diet is over, causing lifelong issues with eating.

Journal It: Hunger Cues

Not all hunger cues are about whether your belly is full! Hunger cues can be physical or psychological. A physical hunger cue is your body telling you it's time to eat; an example of a physical hunger cue is a grumbling stomach. If you're *really* hungry, you might even get cranky or light-headed!

On the other hand, a psychological hunger cue is a mental trigger that makes you want to eat. Not all eating should be based on physical hunger. After all, food is a great pleasure; think how warm and fuzzy you feel at the Thanksgiving table or how special you feel when your mom cooks your favorite homemade dessert! The trouble is that some people end up "eating their feelings" when they feel sad, lonely, or even happy. People might eat as a way to deal with their emotions because they feel uncomfortable talking about them. The trouble with psychological eating is that people often use it as a reason to overeat or even undereat.

Instead of always using food as a temporary fix to make yourself feel better about an emotional situation, explore other healthy ways to release your stress.

Journal It: Hunger Cues (cont)

Call a friend, go for a walk, turn up the music and dance in your living room, paint your nails, read a book, talk to your parents, or enjoy another de-stressing activity. This will help you stay healthy physically and mentally. Learning to recognize and handle your unique physical and psychological hunger cues is a great skill that can help you feel more balanced.

Complete the following sentences in your journal:

I can tell I'm beginning to feel hungry because I experience the following physical cues . . .

If I overeat at dinner, I can tell because I experience the following physical cues . . .

Whenever I feel this emotion, I feel the need to turn toward or away from food to make myself feel better . . .

When I'm dealing with a difficult emotion, I could handle the stress in the following healthy ways . . .

Growing up, I never considered myself fat or thin; I was at a healthy weight for a girl my age. One day, when I was in seventh grade, I was in the locker room changing after gym class when I overheard a classmate exclaim, "A size seven? That's so big!" I was a size seven and I remember leaving gym class feeling as though I was fat. The feelings lingered on for quite some time so I started eating less until I saw the numbers on the scale and my jean size grow smaller. Crash dieting made me thinner, but I was tired and irritable; my

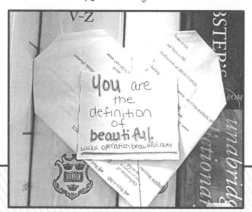

self-image became impaired. I had let one person's voice determine what beautiful looked like and lost myself in their words. It took me years to silence that voice, a voice that continues to be heard today from all sorts of critics that makes so many girls believe that beauty is based on a size. Don't let a number determine your worth. Define beauty for yourself.

Sara, Texas

As a little girl, I used to dream about being in beauty pageants. As a teen and young woman, I entered some locally. I also tried modeling. I believed that was how you achieved success, by how people looked at you. But I was told if I want any kind of career that I would have to lose weight. I nearly killed myself trying. I was so focused on the outside image that my inside got lost. Every day was a struggle to achieve that idea of perfection that I saw in magazines.

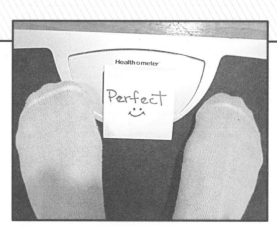

I now focus on how I feel and not how I look. I've learned that beauty is a feeling, not a goal. My idea of perfection is loving myself just the way I am.

Linda, New York

Healthy Eating

Healthy eating is different than dieting for several important reasons. First, healthy eating focuses on providing the awesome, beautiful machine that is your body with nutritious, delicious fuel. With high-quality fuel, your body will run in the most efficient way possible. If your doctor says that you're underweight or overweight according to height/weight charts, healthy eating will help you gain or lose weight the *right* way— slowly and steadily. Even if you're a healthy weight, it's very important to continue to fuel your body with healthy foods! Healthy eating isn't just about appearance; it's about providing your body with food that will actually help you live longer, be stronger, and have more energy.

"Getting enough nutrients and fuel from nutritious foods is important for girls to grow and reach their optimal health," notes Janel Ovrut, a registered dietitian (RD). An RD is an expert on how food impacts the body and advises people on healthy eating. "Healthy eating not only helps you feel good on the inside, but also look good on the outside. It can improve the appearance of your skin, hair, and nails. Healthy eating can even help you be better at sports and do well in school!"

With high-quality fuel, your body will run in the most efficient way possible.

Healthy eating is something you can do for the rest of your life; it's not a quick fix like a diet. This means that healthy eating is not restrictive and won't leave you hungry or unsatisfied. It also means that you don't have to avoid certain foods and can enjoy all your favorite foods—even junk food!— as long as you eat treats every once in a while, not all day, every day.

If you're interested in moving toward healthier eating, don't feel like you have to do a complete food overhaul overnight. Big changes are more likely to stick if you make the switch gradually, and each healthy choice you make adds up over time, no matter how small! Also, healthy eating is often a learning process; after all, you have to figure out how to best apply these tips to your own life.

It took years for you to develop your current eating habits; it might take a while to create new habits. Since you're going to be eating this way for life (healthy eating is a long-term lifestyle—not a quick fix!), it's okay if it takes you a while to figure it out.

Fast Fact: Healthy Eating Summarized

There's a ton of important information below about healthy eating, but here's a quick summary of the most important points:

- When you eat healthy foods, you feel strong and satisfied. Healthy eating will also help you reach or maintain a Happy Weight. Unlike diets, which rarely work in the long-term, healthy eating is something you can do for the rest of your life . . . and you can still enjoy dessert!

- You don't have to be "perfect" in your food choices. Healthy eating is not all-or-nothing. If you eat fast food for lunch, help cook a healthy dinner at home.

- Don't stress out about calories, carbohydrates, or protein. Instead, just eat more Real Food than processed Fake Food.

- Fill your belly with whole-grain cereal, bread, and pasta; fruits and veggies; low-fat dairy; lean meats and beans; and healthy fats from nuts and oils (like olive oil).

- Listen to your body's cues. If you're hungry and in-between meals, eat a healthy snack, like a piece of fruit.

- De-stress by going on a walk, calling a friend, or writing in your journal. Try not to use food to make yourself feel better if you're upset and not hungry.

- Don't skip meals! It's especially important to eat breakfast every day.

Help!: "I keep hearing that I should avoid eating too many processed foods, but I'm not sure what that really means! What should I be eating if I'm not eating processed foods?"

If you think about it, a lot of food that the typical American eats is actually Fake Food—or overly processed food. Fake Foods include ingredients that don't grow in nature and had to be created in a laboratory. Examples of Fake Food include white bread, frozen dinners, sugary breakfast cereals, potato chips, deli meat, frozen pizzas, soda, and cheese dips. Things that are funny colors—like bright-green lollipops— are definitely Fake Foods!

On the other hand, Real Food is food that grows in nature or only has to be minimally processed before being eaten—like apples, green beans, whole wheat bread, meat, beans, or milk.

People eat Fake Foods because they are usually inexpensive, convenient, and taste good. (But Real Food can also be inexpensive, convenient, and taste good, too! It just involves a little more planning.) Real Food often has more vitamins, minerals, and fiber than Fake Food, and Fake Food typically has added salt, sugar, or unhealthy fats. Fake Food might also contain additives or preservatives that help the product stay fresh longer but can harm the body if eaten in excess.

If you think about it, a lot of food that the typical American eats is actually Fake Food—or overly processed.

For example, consider the packaged snack cakes at the gas station. They were baked at a factory and shipped to the store, but how long ago? It might have been weeks, but the snack cakes still taste yummy! On the other hand, if you bake a cake at home using flour, eggs, sugar, and milk, the cake will last only a few days. That's because the Real Food ingredients can last only so long before getting moldy. The packaged snack cake has added chemicals that make it stay fresh way longer than it should.

Fake Food isn't "bad" because the healthy eating doesn't require you to ban any food forever, even processed treats! But dietitians tell us that in order to be healthy, we should eat Fake Foods only in moderation. Most of what we eat should only be processed a little bit to guarantee we're eating the most nutritious foods!

If you're unsure of whether a product is Fake Food or Real Food, ask yourself three simple questions: **Does this food grow in nature?** If not, look at the ingredient list under the nutrition facts label. **Do these ingredients grow in nature?** If there are many ingredients with long, complicated names that you cannot pronounce, odds are that it is a Fake Food. And lastly: **Is this ingredient list way too long?** Fake Foods are filled with preservatives and additives, making for a much longer ingredient list. If the type is too long and too tiny to easily read out loud, odds are it's a Fake Food!

Healthy eating is really about seven things: eating as much Real Food as possible, eating regular meals, eating proper servings, eating a variety of foods, snacking smart, hydrating properly, and enjoying treats in moderation.

HEALTHY EATING TIP #1: Eat Real Food! Every time you choose Real Food over Fake Food, you're getting more important nutrients that your body needs to run properly. Try slowly swapping out most of the packaged or processed foods you eat with foods that are closer to their natural state. It might take a while for your taste buds to adjust, but after a while, you will crave the way healthy Real Food makes your body feel! Here are some suggestions for healthy swaps:

- white rice or white bread for brown rice or whole wheat bread
- chocolate or strawberry milk for low-fat or soy milk
- potato chips for a handful of nuts
- breakfast pastry for oatmeal
- packaged cookies for pieces of fresh fruit, like a banana or an apple
- regular pasta for whole wheat pasta
- chewy Fruit Roll-Ups for raisins or dried apricots
- chips and nacho dip for celery and carrots with hummus or salsa
- soda or sugary iced tea for carbonated water, water with a squirt of lemon, or unsweetened iced tea
- canned fruits and vegetables for fresh or frozen fruits and vegetables (Frozen fruits and vegetables are a great alternative to fresh because the freezing process locks in the nutrients, while canning destroys many nutrients.)
- chicken nuggets for baked chicken
- ranch dressing for olive oil and vinegar

✭ Do It Now! ✭ Learn How to Cook Healthy Foods

Cooking is superfun—and it's not nearly as hard as some people make it seem! If you have a parent who likes to cook, ask if they can teach you. If they aren't a master chef, that's okay—just ask if they can learn how to cook healthy foods with you. Make sure you have your parent's permission before turning on the stove or using big knives! You should also know where the fire extinguisher is located and how to use it, just to be extra safe.

- **Find a Recipe:** You can check out healthy cookbooks or search the Internet for healthy recipes. Great websites to check out include kidshealth.org/teen/recipes, foodnetwork.com, and allrecipes.com. Choose a recipe that isn't too complicated or time-consuming!
- **Prep Yourself:** Wash your hands with warm water and soap before cooking. Also, if you put raw meat or eggs on a plate, in a bowl, or on a cutting board, make sure you wash the dish and utensils before reusing so you don't spread germs.
- **Prep Your Ingredients:** Before you start, review the recipe to make sure you have all the ingredients and tools and understand all the directions. It's helpful to line up all your ingredients on the counter before you begin. If you're using any fresh fruits or vegetables, be sure you thoroughly wash them with warm water before cooking with them or cutting them up to eat.
- **Follow the Recipe . . . or Not:** The first time you make a new dish, it's a good idea to follow the recipe. Once you master the general technique of making homemade spaghetti with whole wheat pasta, you can experiment with adding in extra veggies or swapping out the meatballs for pieces of baked chicken!
- **Learn Healthy Cooking Methods:** Some cooking techniques are healthier than others. Frying vegetables or meats, for example, adds a lot of unhealthy fats to a dish. Healthier alternatives include baking, steaming, or stir-frying—plus many other more advanced techniques! You and your parents can search the Internet for simple phrases like "how to steam vegetables" or "how to bake chicken" to learn more.

✹ Do It Now! ✹ Learn How to Cook Healthy Foods (cont)

- **Create Healthy Sauces:** Choose marinara (red) sauce over cream sauce for a sneaky serving of vegetables with less added fat. Use fresh herbs (like cilantro or basil) instead of extra salt to add flavor. Swap out sour cream with unsweetened plain yogurt. You can even replace vegetable oil with an equal amount of apple sauce when baking cakes or cookies.

- **Cook Extra and Save:** If you plan ahead, you can cook extra portions of your healthy dish and save the leftovers for later. Foods like casseroles or homemade veggie burgers freeze particularly well. Tightly seal glass or plastic containers or plastic bags before putting the food in the freezer to ensure it doesn't get frostbitten!

Fast Fact: Calcium and Iron

Calcium and iron are two important minerals that your body needs to do its job properly! Calcium keeps your bones strong, helps your muscles contract, and is used by your nervous system to send signals between your brain and body. Iron helps your blood carry oxygen to your organs and muscles. "Girls definitely need to make sure they're getting enough iron and calcium," says Janel the RD. "Menstruation [getting your period] increases a girl's need for iron, which can be found in beans, legumes, dark, leafy greens, and lean meats. Eating calcium-rich foods is crucial during puberty, when there is usually rapid bone growth. Meeting calcium needs by eating dairy, dark, leafy greens, and some soy products is especially important during this time so a girl does not end up with weak bones later in life. Some forms of exercise, like jogging, dancing, and tennis, are called 'weight bearing exercises' and also help build bone strength."

HEALTHY EATING TIP #2: Don't Skip Meals! Your body needs fuel all day long to run properly. You know how a warning light comes on when a car is low on gas? Your body does the same thing if you skip meals—it sends you important warning signs, like feeling light-headed or crabby. These signs mean that your body needs more fuel or it will crash! It's especially important that you eat breakfast every day; in fact, people who eat breakfast actually live longer than people who don't.

Another advantage to eating regular meals? It's much easier to make healthy food choices when you aren't starving! "Skipping meals usually cause teens and tweens to grab unhealthy snacks and sweets later on when they're hungry," says Janel the RD. Research shows that people who eat breakfast find it easier to maintain a Happy Weight than people who do not.

HEALTHY EATING TIP #3: Eat Proper Servings! A serving is the recommended amount of the food you should eat at one time. A portion is how much food you choose to eat. One big reason that people struggle with healthy eating is that they simply overeat by consuming portions that are much bigger than the recommended serving. It's easy to do this because portions at restaurants are so big; the amount of pasta you get at a restaurant might actually be four servings instead of one!

As a result, what we see as a "normal" amount of food—even when we're cooking at home—has become exaggerated. Thankfully, most of the foods you buy at the grocery store (with the exception of fruits and vegetables) come with a nutrition facts label. The first line of the nutrition facts tells you the serving size and number of servings in the package. Some packaged foods contain one serving per package; others contain two or three or even fifty! If there is more than one serving in the container, keep in mind that the nutritional facts are for just one serving, not the entire package. Paying attention to the serving size information on the back of packaged foods is one way you can eat healthier.

✴ Do It Now! ✴ Learn How to Read Nutrition Facts

The nutrition facts label tells you tons of important facts about the food. Learning how to read a nutrition facts label can help you make healthier choices! For more information about nutrition facts, visit the Food and Drug Administration's website at fda.gov/food/labelingnutrition.

It can be hard to visualize what a half cup of ice cream looks like in a big bowl! It can also be hard to eat proper servings when you're dining out. Here are some shortcuts you can use to make it easier to eat the correct servings:

- baseball = one serving of a fruit or vegetable
- tennis ball = one serving of ice cream
- golf ball = one serving of trail mix or shelled nuts
- deck of cards = one serving of meat or chicken
- an iPhone = one serving of fish
- two hands cupped together = one serving of cereal
- a Ping-Pong ball = one serving of peanut butter
- computer mouse = one serving of baked potato
- an individual milk carton = one serving of orange juice

HEALTHY EATING TIP #4: Eat a Variety of Foods! Your body needs nutrients from lots of different foods! Many people fall into food ruts and tend to eat the same thing over and over. To stay healthy, it's important to eat a variety of lean meats or vegetarian protein sources (like beans or tofu), dairy, vegetables, fruits, nuts, and whole grains. The American Heart Association recommends that normally active tweens and teens eat the following foods each day (if you're superactive, you'll need more fuel!):

- three servings of low-fat milk or dairy products
- one to two servings (three to five ounces) of meat or beans
- three servings (one and a half cups) of fruits
- two to four servings (one to two cups) of vegetables
- six ounces of grains (one ounce equals one slice of bread, one cup of cereal, or one and a half cups of cooked rice), of which at least half should be whole grains

No one is suggesting you measure out everything you eat and keep a tally to ensure you eat six ounces of grains every day! Instead, remember the general message of the list above and try to incorporate each different food group into every meal; for example, a healthy lunch could include a peanut butter sandwich, an apple, and carrot sticks.

❋ Do It Now! ❋ Pack Your Lunch

Forget that plain old brown paper bag—packing your lunch is suddenly cool again! More and more companies are coming out with stylish, insulated lunch bags so it's easier (and fashionable) to pack your lunch. Plus, a reusable bag (and reusable containers for food instead of plastic bags) is environmentally friendly because it

❊ Do It Now! ❊ Pack Your Lunch (cont)

reduces waste. Reusable bags are available at retail stores such as Target and Walmart.

Packing your lunch is typically much healthier than buying it at school or going out to eat. Packing lunch the night before and storing it in the fridge until the morning will ensure you don't run out of time—or just plain forget—to pack your lunch as you dash off to school. Here are some quick suggestions for packed lunches.

Main Dishes

- whole wheat sandwich with all-natural peanut butter, low-sodium deli meat, or hummus. Add spinach or tomato slices for an extra serving of veggies!
- brown rice with canned black, pinto, or kidney beans or chickpeas. Add salsa for some extra flavor.
- whole wheat wraps stuffed with grilled or baked chicken, hummus, or beans with a variety of veggies and mustard or ketchup. Roll the wrap up with aluminum foil and peel away the foil as you eat for a mess-free meal.
- vegetable, chicken noodle, or your other favorite soup (in a thermos container to keep it warm)
- cottage cheese with peeled orange slices or strawberries
- taco salad with lettuce, corn, salsa, beans or chicken strips, and a few tortilla chips
- cold pasta salad with whole wheat pasta, veggies, cheese, and Italian salad dressing

Side Dishes

- whole fruit, such as an apple, banana, pear, or orange
- veggies, such as carrots, celery, grape tomatoes, or raw broccoli. Bring a small container of hummus or salsa for dipping!
- string cheese or yogurt
- ants on a log (celery with peanut butter and raisins in the middle!)

Help!: "I know I should eat a variety of foods to be healthy, but I really, really hate vegetables. They're disgusting! How can anyone like them?"

Did you know that there are over ten thousand taste buds in your mouth? Taste buds have special receptors that tell your brain information about the food in your mouth. Taste buds say, "This popcorn is salty!" or "This watermelon is so sweet." If you open your mouth and look at your tongue in the mirror, you can actually see some of your taste buds—they look like little bumps.

When you're a baby, your taste buds are supersensitive. As you grow up, you lose some taste buds and some of the remaining receptors don't experience tastes as strongly. When you're an older adult, you might only have five thousand taste buds! This means that a food you tried and hated when you were five years old might actually taste different and more delicious now!

Vegetables can be prepared many different healthy ways—like steaming, stir-frying, or roasting—and each technique makes the veggie taste different! You can also add spices or sauces to veggies to make them taste different. For example, if you hate raw carrots, try this easy recipe: Chop a couple of rinsed and peeled carrots into one-inch segments, rub the carrots in a mixture of one tablespoon maple syrup and one-half tablespoon cinnamon, place on a greased cookie dish, and bake at 400 degrees for twenty minutes.

It's also easy to "sneak" veggies into your meals. You can add chopped red and green peppers to pasta sauces or mash steamed broccoli or cauliflower into regular mashed potatoes. You can add a handful of raw spinach to the blender when making smoothies—it will turn your strawberry smoothie bright-green, but you won't be able to taste it at all!

Don't completely write off certain foods—give them another shot or find new ways to prepare them! You might discover that you do love vegetables, after all.

HEALTHY EATING TIP #5: Snack Smart! "Tweens and teens will find that as they get older, they may need more food to fuel their growing bodies, so small snacks between meals may be necessary," says Janel the RD. Plus, snack time is the perfect time to sneak in fruits and vegetables—after all, tweens and teens should eat three servings of fruits and two to four servings of vegetables a day. Here are some healthy snack ideas to keep your energy levels sky-high.

- carrot sticks and peanut butter
- a peach and cottage cheese
- a banana and a serving of Greek yogurt
- an apple and a slice of cheddar cheese
- peanut butter on toast
- raw broccoli dipped in hummus
- grapes and string cheese
- one serving of nuts
- granola bars (healthy brands include Kashi, Clif, and Larabar)
- whole grain serving of bread with one serving of milk

The most important part of snacking smart? Being prepared! Take some time in the morning to think about whether you'll need a snack while at school and plan accordingly. "Girls should prepare snacks that they can easily stash in their backpack, purse, or locker so they don't have to head to the vending machine or fast-food joint when they're hungry while on the go," says Janel. "Cold foods like cheese or yogurt should be kept in a backpack or locker with a freezer pack so they stay fresh."

HEALTHY EATING TIP #6: Hydrate Properly! Dehydration occurs when a person loses more water than they are taking in. Dehydration can be sudden and severe; for example, if you're playing soccer on a hot, summer day and sweating buckets, but you never take a break to drink anything, you might start to feel light-headed and faint! But not drinking enough water on a daily basis can hurt your body's ability to function in small ways, too. Water helps us digest our food, moisturizes our skin, and keeps our brains awake and focused.

You can hydrate your body by drinking a glass of water with every meal, drinking water when you play sports, and eating fruits and vegetables, which also contain a lot of water. A simple trick to tell if you've had enough water to drink is to look at the color of your urine after you go to the bathroom; if it's dark yellow, you need to drink more! If it's pale yellow or clear, you're properly hydrating.

Fast Fact: Water, Water Everywhere

Your body is approximately 60 percent water! Isn't that crazy?

Remember that many drinks count as Fake Food. "Water is the only beverage teens and tweens need to hydrate their bodies and quench their thirst," says Janel the RD. "Soda is full of sugar and empty calories, which means that it contains a lot of calories that your body may not need, and soda also doesn't have any vitamins, minerals, protein, or fiber." Janel says that sports drinks and enhanced vitamin beverages are like soda in disguise! "They are also high in sugar and unnecessary calories," she explains. "It is best to get calories, energy, and nutrients from foods, and stick to water for hydration."

Fruit juice is a fun way to sneak in a serving of fruit while hydrating, but make sure you check the label first! Look for the phrase "100 percent juice" or check the ingredient list to make sure there's no added sugar. "Fruit is naturally sweet!" says Janel, who also recommends limiting your juice consumption to four to eight ounces a day.

HEALTHY EATING TIP #7: Enjoy Treats in Moderation! The best thing about healthy eating is that there is room for treats. This isn't a diet, remember? This is a way you can eat for life, and life just wouldn't be the same without the occasional slice of cake, candy bar, salty chips, or other treats! The key is to enjoy treats in moderation, which means you eat a serving of a treat a few times a week, but not big desserts every day. If you have a sweet tooth, you could eat a small treat every single day to satisfy yourself so you don't feel deprived (because who wants to feel like that?!). For example, you could eat a few squares of dark chocolate after dinner every day.

Help!: "I really want to change my eating habits and become healthier, but my family isn't on board. My parents buy unhealthy foods and think it's weird that I want to eat more vegetables and whole grains. What do I do? I can't buy our groceries or force my parents to change!"

Food and exercise are very touchy topics for some people, and it's not unusual for parents to think their children are judging them if the child tries to change what's in the family's grocery cart. Parents might secretly feel ashamed that they don't know how to buy healthy foods at the store or cook healthy meals. They might also feel responsible if their child is struggling with their weight. Plus, some people think that eating healthy food is boring, yucky, or expensive. (It's not!)

Parents might secretly feel ashamed that they don't know how to buy healthy foods at the store or cook healthy meals.

Instead of pointing your finger at your parents and saying, "*You* need to stop buying *me* unhealthy foods," try pulling together everyone in the family as a team. A good way to start the conversation is, "I'm really interested in being healthier and learning to cook. Do you think we could learn how to do this together?" If your parents are concerned it will be too time-consuming, offer to go grocery shopping with them or suggest that they let you cook dinner a few times a week. If they fear healthy eating is too expensive, sit down at the computer together and search the Internet for "inexpensive and healthy recipes"— there are many healthy dishes that cost way less than getting takeout or pizza delivered.

If you bring lunch to school, tell your parents that you'll take over the responsibility of packing lunch if they will buy you healthier alternatives. "If your parents are not willing to bring healthy food home, you can look into buying lunch at school if there are healthy options available," says Janel the RD.

Instead of pointing your finger at your parents and saying, "*You* need to stop buying *me* unhealthy foods," try pulling together everyone in the family as a team.

Remember that small changes add up over time and that new eating habits are more likely to stick when they are implemented gradually. Even if your parents aren't 100 percent on board right away, they'll come around!

✺ Do It Now! ✺ Learn More about Healthy Eating

Entire books have been written on the subject of healthy eating; remember that this chapter is just an introduction to the idea! If you want to learn more about healthy eating, talk to your parents or research healthy eating topics on the Internet. (Just be careful to only accept advice from a trusted website; if you aren't sure, ask your parents.)

"You can also talk to your doctor about healthy eating or ask for a referral to see a dietitian," says Janel the RD. "A dietitian can answer your nutrition questions and discuss ways to make healthy choices. A health or physical education teacher can provide information on overall health and fitness, so be sure to use your school as a resource, too."

Growing up, I didn't do what I loved but rather what everyone else told me to do. I was a dancer, however, I would cry to my mom on the phone saying I didn't want to go to dance class. Most of my friends dropped out already and I didn't want to be the only one there. Eventually my mom gave in and I stopped dancing. I lost one of my passions because I was afraid to be different. In the middle of my sophomore year I struggled with my group of friends. Over that summer, I spent time discovering myself in the kitchen. Baking, photography, and writing became passions I never knew I had; passions that I will never let go just because other people think I am different. Now I have a cooking blog, which has taught me that creating my own path doesn't make me weird or an outcast, but rather unique and interesting. I love what I do and can't express what it has brought me: a future, a new perspective on life, and a hobby.

In high school, I also noticed a lot of negative talk and Fat Talk. Even though I was a healthy weight, I too began to see myself as "fat," too! Over the past few months, I have begun to see that what I once saw as "fat" is actually muscle! Muscle that carries me through 9.3-mile runs! Muscle that inspires me to try new challenges every day. Muscle that gave me the ability to jump, play sports, and be happy.

If you ever doubt what you are doing, don't . . . dare to be different.

Chelsey, New Jersey

Be yourself, and live your life the way you want. Don't let other people get in the way of your dream! Because if you believe in yourself, your dreams can come true!

Mackenzie, Indiana

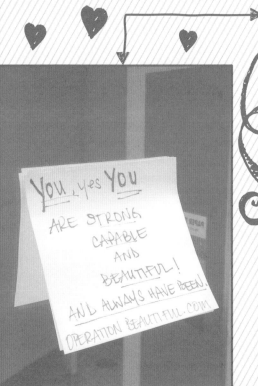

On a whim, I went to see a nutritionist who taught me about healthy eating. For the first time, I started to understand my body's relationship to food—to see food as fuel and to recognize the difference between physical hunger and emotional hunger. As I learned to connect what I ate to how I felt, everything came together. I began to see more clearly what my body needed to feel energized and for my mind to be focused; my yoga practice deepened and I started to cultivate mindfulness and attention more easily off the mat; and I found the real meaning of health: being connected to myself and nourishing my mind as well as my body. Now I know that feeling tired doesn't have to be my "normal." Now, I run, ride, and climb, I say "yes" to physical challenges, and I feel like an athlete. I also cook with Real Foods, read labels, check in with myself to understand the nature of my cravings, and I finally feel like I know what it is for me to be healthy.

Debbie, California

My favorite thing to do is play basketball because it's fun to work with your friends and your teammates. I want to eat more fruits and vegetables so I can be healthier. I know that eating healthy foods will help me with running and help me be a better athlete.

People tell me I'm nice and caring. Whenever someone is hurt, I help them. I try to take care of everyone like they are my brother or sister. I don't like the way the media portrays beauty. It's all about looks—looking at how pretty or sexy someone is—which isn't how you should look at someone. You should look through their eyes and at their heart.

Girls can be so hard on each other. They are very prideful and can be very rude and have big mood swings sometimes. Girls start to feel left out or they start to compete with each other. This sometimes comes from insecurity and they don't have someone to tell them how proud they are of them. Operation Beautiful can help by reminding these girls that they can be themselves and be happy. They don't have to feel like they are alone—they see a note and feel beautiful.

Ashlyn, Florida

In middle school, I felt like I didn't stand out. I wasn't the prettiest, the most popular, the most athletic, or the smartest. So what was so wonderful about being me? I wanted to be anyone but me. I was my own worst enemy. These negative thoughts kept building up to the point where I developed an anxiety disorder.

During this time, I constantly struggled with nagging thoughts about life and not measuring up to what was expected of me, about what others thought of me, about making a fool of myself, about being ordinary. I felt a constant pressure of being perfect in every way possible, which I have now come to realize is beyond impossible. And more importantly . . . it's undesirable. Flaws make us unique, and there is nothing interesting about a perfect person.

Even though I was just a teen, I started living a healthier lifestyle. I became passionate about running and loved my body enough to provide it with the most nutritious food. Why couldn't I do the same for who I was as a person? This new lifestyle opened up my eyes to what was missing in my life before. Respect for myself. Finally, it hit me. No one is any better than me. Repeat it a million times if you need to, but if one thing is true in this world it is that. Don't let anyone else make you believe otherwise!

I still occasionally get negative thoughts . . . I mean, who doesn't? But whenever that happens, I think about Operation Beautiful and remind myself just how awesome it is to be me.

Natalia, Michigan

Sweat, Beautiful Sweat!

Your body was made to move, run, dance, jump, and experience life to the fullest. Exercise doesn't have to be a chore—think of exercise as giving your body a big "thank you!" hug. Like healthy eating, exercise is one way you can express respect for your beautiful body. It's also an awesome self-esteem booster. So let's get moving!

Work It Out

A lot of people wrinkle up their noses when they hear the word *exercise*. Exercise has somehow gotten a reputation for being a dreaded chore. Other people think exercise just isn't for them—it's too hard or they feel so out of shape that they don't bother trying.

Word Up Exercise

Think exercise only happens when you're trapped in a dark, smelly gym? Not so! Exercise is anything that gets your body moving and your heart pumping. Exercise includes biking around your neighborhood, playing tag with friends, participating in after-school sports, dancing to your favorite songs in your bedroom, and walking your dog.

As you just learned, healthy eating is so important because it provides your body with the fuel it needs to function properly. Exercise is just as important as healthy eating! Exercise makes you stronger, both mentally and physically. It also boosts your self-esteem, decreases the odds that you'll get sick, relieves stress, and can even help you make new friends. Exercise can also help you reach or maintain a Happy Weight and feel more confident about your body. Plus, exercise is actually quite fun—and if you think it's not, you just haven't discovered the perfect exercise for *you*!

Exercise is just as important as healthy eating!

Basically, exercise has unfairly earned a bad reputation, but Operation Beautiful knows the truth—sweat might be stinky, but it's also a very beautiful thing.

Unfortunately, less and less girls are having fun breaking a sweat than ever before. Just like there are many environmental factors—or factors outside of your control— contributing to our nation's unhealthy eating habits, there are environmental factors that influence why we don't get enough exercise. Girls used to be able to count on recess or P.E. to provide them with an hour of exercise each day, but many schools have cut recess

time for reasons like they want to save money or they just don't have enough space. Some schools have also been forced to cut funding—the money they spend for an activity—for after-school sports.

And while technology is an awesome thing, a side effect of the Internet, smart phones, television, and video games is that people spend a lot more time staring at a screen than they did even just a few years ago. The trouble is that, more often than not, kids and adults are choosing electronic experiences over real-life activities. Instead of grabbing our bikes and exploring our neighborhood with friends, we're sitting in a darkened room playing video games. (But there are also new video games that require the player to use her body as the controller; these games are actually a great form of exercise because you spend time jumping, dancing, and ducking instead of sitting.)

Your body isn't designed to surf the Internet from your comfy couch.

It's designed to MOVE! Some people are afraid of exercise because they don't *feel* strong or capable, but a really cool thing about exercise is that your body responds to it so quickly. After just one week of regular exercise, you'll see a huge improvement in your abilities. After another week, you'll be able to run circles around the old you. Remember that strong is beautiful—so get movin'!

Fast Fact: Screen Time Overload

Can you believe that six to eleven year olds spend about twenty-eight hours a week in front of the TV? That's like a part-time job! Amazingly, the average tween and teen spends more than seven and a half hours a day looking at a phone, computer, or television screen.

Before exercising, make sure you do three important things:

- **Stretch and Warm Up:** You want to ease into exercise, not shock your body with rigorous activity! Stretching and warming up gets your muscles, tendons, and ligaments (which all attach to your bones or to one another) loose and ready for action. You can warm up by doing jumping jacks, jogging in place, walking briskly, or slowly dancing around. It's also a good idea to loosen your joints by making big, slow circles with your arms, neck, hips, and legs. When you stretch, remember to slowly reach—do not bounce! Bouncing can cause injury and pain. If you want to learn more about warming up and stretching, check out the fitness resource websites listed at the end of this chapter.
- **Eat a Snack if Necessary:** If you exercise on a full tummy, you might get a bad cramp. But if you exercise on an empty stomach, you might not have the necessary calories available to fuel your body through your workout!

Your body needs quality calories to help it do the exercises, so if it's been more than a few hours since the last time you ate, have a small snack before exercising. Pre-workout snack ideas include a handful of nuts, a slice of toast with peanut butter, a glass of milk, or fresh fruit.

- **Grab Your Water Bottle:** It is extremely important that you drink water while exercising or you could end up dehydrated. Also, staying hydrated actually improves your athletic ability, so you'll be able to run faster, jump higher, and play longer when you have a water bottle in hand.

Help!: "I really want to become healthier, but I am superembarrassed to exercise or play sports in front of other people! I feel like everyone is criticizing me and staring."

You are not alone; workout embarrassment is a very common problem. People might feel embarrassed because they are trying something new and feel uncomfortable in the situation. It's important to remember that usually no one else is paying as much attention to you as you think. Other people are too focused on themselves! For example, if you're shy to play soccer because you have to run around in front of others, don't stress out—the other players are probably too busy running after the ball to notice if your shirt rides up.

Also, don't assume that people who are looking at you are thinking negatively about you. They might be pondering their next big test, staring off into space, or admiring your nice shirt. And who knows—they might be staring at you because they are impressed you're trying something new! But if someone really is teasing you, it's bullying. Talk to a parent or teacher about the situation.

If you're trying a new activity and have no idea if you're doing it right, just take a deep breath and relax. Asking a coach or trainer for assistance can help you develop the skills to feel like a pro. By opening up to others and admitting that you're a first-timer, you might develop some great friendships. Use humor to lighten the situation, "Hey, Coach—I really want to try playing softball, but I really have no idea how to catch a ball in a mitt. I'll drop it like a buttered watermelon! Do you think you can show me how?"

Here are some positive mantras to repeat in your head as you venture into new activities:

- Everyone starts somewhere.
- I will embrace being a newbie and discovering new skills for the first time.
- Everyone is too wrapped up in their own stuff to care about mine.
- Just because someone is looking at me, it doesn't mean they are thinking anything negative.
- It takes courage to try something new; I am so strong!
- How will I ever know what I'm capable of unless I try?

Instead of thinking of exercise as a chore, consider that it's really a chance to have fun and relax. Exercise is a great stress reliever and can be the best part of your day. If you're mad about something that happened at school or home, you can go for a bike ride or run and take your frustrations out in a healthy way. You can also use exercise as a chance to catch up with friends—instead of sitting in a dark movie theater with your best friend, go for a long walk around your neighborhood and actually have a chance to talk to each other!

Notice that the gym hasn't been mentioned at all! Gyms are convenient and staffed with professionals who can show you how to use all the equipment (just ask!). A lot of people love going to the gym, but you don't *need* a gym to exercise. You can exercise in your neighborhood, at a park, or even in your bedroom.

Here are four ways you can incorporate more fun exercises into your life, even if your family doesn't belong to a gym:

- **Exercise Alone:** Do you feel like people are always bugging you, asking you for things, or interrupting your thoughts? Exercise is a great way to get "me time." Get your solo exercise fix by going on a walk or run, dancing to music, riding your bike, or doing a workout DVD in your living room.
- **Exercise with a Team:** Consider signing up for an after-school or extracurricular sport team. Some teams are competitive and others are just for fun. If you're new to exercise or to that particular sport, join a team or activity that welcomes everyone. Many activities encourage complete newbies who want to learn new skills to join, so don't feel like you have to be a pro before joining a group! Maybe you can even convince a friend to try it out with you.

  If your immediate reaction to this suggestion is: "But I hate sports," consider that there's life beyond the "traditional" sports like baseball and soccer. Consider karate, track-and-field, badminton, fencing, Ultimate Frisbee, golf, swimming, volleyball, rowing, gymnastics, cheerleading, or dance. If your school doesn't offer the activity you're interested in, search the Internet for after-school groups in your community.
- **Exercise with Your Friends:** Instead of watching television, playing video games, or shopping at the mall, go for a run or bike ride with your friends. You'll end up talking more than you did on the couch! No one is too old to play games—games like four square, hopscotch, and jump rope are actually great workouts! You could even organize a day-long kickball or softball tournament with a large group of friends.
- **Exercise with Your Family:** Having a workout buddy makes regular exercise a lot more enjoyable. Try recruiting your mom, dad, brother, or sister to work out with you every day. You can go on family walks after dinner or shoot hoops before school. You can even incorporate exercise into family vacations by planning a group hike.

✸ Do It Now! ✸ Learn How to Run

Running is an excellent form of exercise: It's fun, and you can run almost anywhere. (As long as there are sidewalks!) Running can seem really hard when you first start, but the cool thing about running is that you'll see improvements in your endurance quickly. And who doesn't like instant gratification?!

Before you begin running, make sure you have the right kind of shoes on. It's important to wear sneakers designed for running, not flimsy tennis shoes. Your bones and joints need the extra cushioning provided by running sneakers. You might also want to wear special clothes that are designed not to soak up sweat and a sports bra, although this gear isn't required.

It's important to find a safe place to run. Running outside is really fun because there's lots to look at, but you want to stay away from traffic and run in a safe neighborhood or park. Running with a buddy is your safest bet. If you're running alone, always tell an adult where you'll be running and when you'll be back. You should also carry a school identification card with your emergency contact information written on the back; if you don't have an ID card, you can write the information on a piece of paper and slip it in your pocket. If you have a cell phone, take it with you on the run so you can call for help in an emergency or if you get lost. You can also run indoors on the treadmill; just make sure you know how to properly use the machine before getting on!

A lot of people think they are "failing" if they take a break to walk. But guess what? Walking is awesome and doing a run/walk combination (when you run for two minutes and walk for one, for example) can actually make you faster overall. That's right—you can actually be *faster* by taking walking breaks!

That's because walking gives you a mental boost and recharges your body.

When you first start, aim to run/walk for at least twenty minutes. Use a watch to time your run/walk combinations and try to keep a steady rhythm. Learning how to pace yourself—which means keeping a steady rhythm instead of always sprinting, getting tired, jogging, sprinting, getting tired, and jogging again—takes practice, but just listen to your body! After doing several twenty-minute run/walk intervals a week, you'll be able to slowly (over many weeks) extend the overall exercise time and reduce the amount of walking that you do. Eventually, you might not need to walk at all if you don't want to!

One way to get over the walking hump is to pick a landmark in the distance—like a light pole or street corner—and run until you get to that point. Take a walking break and pick out a new landmark to run toward when you're ready. Having a goal makes running a lot easier!

You can sign up for a 5K race (3.1 miles, or about forty-five minutes of run/walking) to help keep yourself motivated. It takes most people two to three months to get ready for a 5K. Consider asking one of your parents if they'd like to train for a race with you! Remember to always run at your own pace, which means you run or walk at a speed that is comfortable for you, if you're running with a buddy that is naturally faster than you. If you're faster than your buddy, run at their pace and encourage them!

For more information, search the Internet for the "Couch to 5K program." Also be sure to talk to your doctor and parents before beginning any kind of workout program. If you feel any injuries coming on from running, it's important that you take a few days off and talk to your doctor if the pain sticks around.

Fast Fact: Exercise Makes You Happier

When you exercise, your body releases natural hormones into your blood stream. One of the hormones is called endorphin. Endorphins actually make you feel happier, more confident, and in a better mood. So if you're feeling sad, write yourself an Operation Beautiful note, lace up your sneakers, and go for a walk!

The big question is how much exercise do we really need? The answer might surprise you—the government recommends that tweens and teens move their bodies for an hour every day! If that seems like a lot, don't feel intimidated. First, you don't have to do it all at once—you can break it into fifteen-minute or thirty-minute chunks. Second, everyday activity can count as exercise! Choosing to take the stairs instead of the elevator, carrying heavy bags of groceries up the stairs, dancing to music, raking the lawn, and even walking the dog all count toward the hour of exercise we each need every day.

Don't let yourself fall into the all-or-nothing trap with exercise, either! One hour a day can seem overwhelming if you don't regularly exercise right now, so start off with small goals. Talk to your parents about your desire to fit in more physical activity and suggest going on a family walk before or after dinner. Even if you start off with twenty minutes a day—well, that's twenty minutes more than yesterday, right?

A lot of people have trouble maintaining an exercise routine because they dive in headfirst and try to do it all right away. Just like it's challenging to learn healthy eating habits, it can be hard to figure out how exercise can fit into your daily life. Instead of making yourself crazy trying to do it all, pledge to make small changes each week. Over time, your small efforts will add up to something amazing!

- Go for a walk every day after dinner.
- Ask if your church or temple offers fitness classes.
- Walk to school or the store whenever possible.
- Play active video games like Wii Fit or Kinect for Xbox.
- Throw a dance party in your living room.
- Watch YouTube videos on introductory yoga and learn positions like downward dog, warrior, tree, and triangle.
- Play fun outdoor games like capture the flag.
- Go on a hike through a local park.
- Play tag with your dog.
- Jump rope—it's harder than it looks!
- Check your television to see if on-demand exercise videos are available.
- Jump on a trampoline.

Above all else—be safe with exercise! Exercise should be challenging, but it shouldn't feel like you're injuring your body. The old saying "no pain, no gain" could not be further from the truth! If a particular motion hurts, stop immediately. If you feel dizzy or light-headed, experience chest pains, or have trouble breathing, you should also stop immediately and tell an adult.

 Journal It: My Favorite Exercises

Some people like running, other people like dancing. Some girls love to do push-ups, and others prefer to play outside. Everyone is different, and there's truly a workout to suit all tastes. Journal a list of your favorite workouts by completing the following sentences.

My favorite workouts include . . .

Fun activities that I'd love to try include . . .

❋ Do It Now! ❋ Learn More about Healthy Exercise

If you're looking to learn more about healthy exercise, check out these excellent websites:

Kidnetic at kidnetic.com

Girls' Health at girlshealth.gov/fitness/

Young Women's Health at
        youngwomenshealth.org/nutrition_menu.html#fitness

Teen's Health at kidshealth.org/teen/food_fitness/

Web MD at teens.webmd.com/aerobic-exercise-for-teens

I like all sports; in fact, I've played almost every girl sport except basketball. My favorite sport would have to be softball. I have been playing softball for almost five years now! When I was in elementary school, I loved recess. Now that I'm in middle school, we don't have recess. I miss it!

Madison, North Carolina

It's the message behind the hands that make them beautiful!

Beautiful to me is a deaf person playing a challenging sport like basketball. In basketball, I had a hard time hearing and understanding what my teammates were saying. During my freshman and sophomore year, my coach rarely put me in the game, even though I went to practice every day and sacrificed my time to improve. It was a tough two years for me because everybody thought that deaf people couldn't play basketball.

But during the summertime, my friend's mom told the coaches to let her daughter and I play in the games because it was not fair for us to work hard and not play. When the game came, our coaches put us in the game and we scored some points. I was happy to score six points at the three-point line because I showed my team and coaches that deaf people can play basketball.

It is beautiful to be deaf because you may not play exactly like other people, but you can play it your way. I'm the only deaf basketball player on my team, and that was my most beautiful moment ever!

Nicole (with her friends Brianah, Natasha, Darius, and Christian), Pennsylvania

For me, middle school wasn't the easiest time. Among my friends I always felt like the pudgy one. When I realized I didn't look like all the other girls in my grade, I became very self-conscious—I started wearing baggy clothes to hide my perceived imperfections. I shrunk into myself a little, and it became hard to make new friends. My mom (who is now one of my best friends) decided I needed an after-school activity and put me in ballet class. I was horrified! Tights and leotards!? Everyone was going to see my body! But I fell in love with ballet. And here's the thing about finding an activity you're passionate about—you have an opportunity to throw yourself into something wonderful and forget about being so self-conscious. After a year, not only did I lose a little bit of weight in a healthy way, but I became more confident in myself. I could walk into a classroom with my head held high. And that's the key—confidence. You can face anything if you know who you are and what makes you . . . YOU.

Susannah, Virginia

today you are you, that is truer than true. there is no one alive who is youer than you!!
~Dr. Seuss

www.operationbeautiful.com

You have one body Start LOVIN' IT!

Isabelle, Ohio

I was kind of feeling down during photography class because the teacher told us to do a self-portrait assignment. But then I found this enlightening note in the bathroom of my school. It changed the way I thought about everything that had been on my mind. There will always be a time in your life when someone tells you or you think that you're not good enough, too fat, too skinny, not smart enough, not fun, not exciting, or not worth the time. On the inside, these words and thoughts hurt us, and those lies that are told make us think and do things that are not good for ourselves. Have confidence and love your body the way it is! No one is perfect, so love what you are and be proud!

Rebecca, New York

Liana, New York

Conclusion

People sometimes ask me if I truly believe that an Operation Beautiful note can actually make a difference. Our world is filled with negative messages: from the media, advertisers, and sometimes even from our parents and friends. These messages are drilled into our brains over and over again until we start to believe that we're not good enough, not pretty enough, not smart enough, not funny enough, or just not . . . *enough*. In our image-focused society, it's hard for many people to believe that one kind word from a stranger would even be heard over the roar of all this negativity.

But negativity is a whisper; positivity is a shout. As you've read, Operation Beautiful has a surprisingly strong effect on the way people see themselves and the world. Nothing is more uplifting than entering a public bathroom, opening a library book, or flipping over a box of cereal and finding a kind word from a stranger. These little notes make a difference every day: healing the scars of bullying, encouraging healthy and balanced living, and promoting a message of inner beauty, not Photoshopped flawlessness. And while Operation Beautiful notes are left in random spots, the magical thing is that each note is destined for someone special to find. Your note might be discovered by a girl who just needed a smile or a woman who is desperately looking for a sign—any sign!—that it's all going to work out. Your note might literally save someone's life.

In our image-focused society, it's hard for many people to believe that one kind word from a stranger would even be heard over the roar of all this negativity.

When I stuck the first Operation Beautiful note on a bathroom mirror,

I had no idea what I was starting. How could I have realized that my note would snowball into thousands of notes, posted all over the world? My first note was only the beginning of countless other blizzards of positivity: Each person who posts an Operation Beautiful note kick-starts the movement all over again. Who knows who will find your Operation Beautiful note. Who knows how many notes that person will post. And whose life will be transformed.

The secret to Operation Beautiful is that while finding a note is special, the truly amazing thing is being the note writer. When we write Operation Beautiful notes, we are really telling *ourselves* the positive and kind messages. Operation Beautiful ignites a revolution in our hearts. The more often you write Operation Beautiful notes, the easier it becomes to tune out all the negativity and believe that you are truly beautiful and unique.

You are more powerful than you realize. Not only can your actions positively impact other people, but you have the power to transform your own life. Life does not happen *to* you; you make life happen *for* you. If you set your mind to something, you can accomplish it. If you want to be a writer, write. If you want to play soccer, do it. If you're not sure what you want to do, try anything and everything! The world is at your feet— you just have to seize the opportunity to become the girl you want to be. There might be setbacks along the way, but that's okay—success might happen on the second or third or even forty-third try!

Life does not happen *to* you; you make life happen *for* you.

We don't have control over what other people say or do. All we control is the way we choose to react to negative forces. You can be positive or negative in the face of any situation. (And—trust me—being positive is so much better.) The greatest gifts you can give yourself are positivity, forgiveness, and hope. Not only are these gifts free and limitless, but they have the power to transform the most horrible of situations into something bearable. I know it's hard to feel that you have control when you're a girl who has to listen to parents and teachers. You ultimately have control over how you view the world . . . and attitude is everything.

My greatest hope is that within these pages, you've discovered that Operation Beautiful is more than a little scrap of paper. Operation Beautiful is a powerful reminder that there's a light inside you, and nothing can put it out. Too often we waste energy looking for answers outside of ourselves, but the truth is that you already possess the power to live the incredible life you deserve. Everything you need is already inside of you.

You are beautiful in so many amazing ways.

Glossary

Action Plan: describes what you want, the steps required to reach your goal, and solutions to possible obstacles.

Assertive Behavior: a form of communication that lets others know how you feel without putting them on the defensive. Assertive behavior is more effective than being passive (letting other people take advantage of you and not telling them how you really feel) or aggressive (being too angry). Take a deep breath before making an assertive statement and try to begin your sentences with the word *I*; for example, assertive statements often begin with "I feel . . ." or "I don't like it when . . ."

Body Mass Index (BMI): compares your height to your weight while accounting for your age and gender. BMI lets the doctor know if your weight falls into the underweight, healthy weight, overweight, or obese (which means very overweight) range.

Body Type: a way to categorize different body shapes and sizes. The most general body types include apple, pear, banana, and hourglass; however, you can be a combination of two body types or fall somewhere in between two types. All body types are beautiful and unique.

Bullying: teasing, hitting, gossiping, spreading rumors, rolling your eyes, playing keep-away with someone else's things, and/or being mean. Bullying can occur between strangers, friends, or even family members (like a brother bullying his sister).

Calorie: a measurement of how much energy is in food. In order to run properly, your body needs a certain number of calories every day. It's important to eat calories that provide a lot of the nutrients your body needs, like calories from lean meat, beans, low-fat dairy, fruits, vegetables, and nuts, instead of eating too many calories from junk food, like fast food or soda.

Crash Diet: a strict style of eating that usually results in weight loss, but for only a short time. Diets, unless recommended by a doctor, are typically unhealthy because they label some foods as "bad" and promote "all-or-nothing" thinking. Most people gain back the weight that they lost on a diet.

Cyberbullying: bullying that happens over the Internet or on the phone. Cyberbullies use chat rooms, blogs, Facebook, or other social network sites to publicly humiliate or harass other kids. E-mail, text messages, instant messages, and direct messages might be used to "trick" someone into revealing a secret.

Exercise: any activity that gets your body moving and your heart pumping. Exercise includes biking around your neighborhood, playing tag with friends, participating in after-school sports, dancing to your favorite songs in your bedroom, and walking your dog.

Deceptive Advertising: commercials that try to trick you into liking a product or believing it works. Marketers often use Photoshop to make products or models appear "better"; for example, one type of deceptive advertising is Photoshopping away a model's wrinkles in an advertisement for anti-wrinkle cream.

Fake Food: Fake Foods include ingredients that don't grow in nature and had to be created in a laboratory. Examples of Fake Foods include white bread, frozen dinners, sugary breakfast cereals, potato chips, deli meat, frozen pizza, soda, and cheese dips.

Fat Talk: negative noise about your appearance. You can Fat Talk out loud to other people, and you can also have Fat Talk thoughts in your own mind. Fat Talk isn't limited to the feeling of being "too big," and it has nothing to do with your actual size or weight. Fat Talk is really about how you feel about yourself on the inside. Many people Fat Talk because they believe they aren't good enough because of their appearance.

Fat Talk–Free Pledge: a promise to stop Fat Talking. You can challenge yourself to stop Fat Talking or do it in a group with your friends or family members.

Flower Cutter: an overwhelmingly negative person who attempts to "cut down" other people to feel better than them.

Gender Stereotype: social norms about what is acceptable behavior or appearance for women and men. For example, a gender stereotype is that boys like to play with trucks and girls like to play with dolls.

Happy Weight: a healthy weight that you reach through healthy eating and fun exercise. It's the weight that your body naturally maintains when you eat healthy foods and enjoy treats in moderation.

Healthy Ideal: the opposite of the Thin Ideal or the Muscular Ideal, which say that girls and boys have to look a certain way to be attractive. The Healthy Ideal focuses on being the healthiest version of yourself through balanced eating, exercise, and positive thinking. The Healthy Ideal comes in many different shapes and sizes, from thin to full and short to tall. There is no "one size fits all" approach to being healthy—healthy looks different on different people because we all have different body types.

Hunger Cue: a signal to eat. Hunger cues can be physical or psychological. A physical hunger cue is your body telling you it's time to eat; an example of a physical hunger cue is a grumbling stomach. A psychological hunger cue is a mental trigger that makes you want to eat. Some people want to eat when they feel sad, angry, or happy.

Materialism: a focus on having "stuff" like new clothes, gadgets, or toys. It's better to value your relationships and positive qualities like kindness or listening skills over having lots of things.

Media Literacy: technique that helps people study and evaluate images or ideas presented in the media.

Muscular Ideal: the idea of beauty for boys and men that the media has created over time through pictures in magazines and commercials on television. The Muscular Ideal often says that men should have six-pack abs and a full head of hair.

Negative Noise: negative self-talk, either out loud or in your thoughts. Negative noise can be about your looks, intelligence, personality, or abilities. You can also experience negative noise from other people; bullying is an example of negative noise from others.

Perfectionist: someone who believes that anything less than perfect is unacceptable. Perfectionists often strive to be productive and meet deadlines. However, perfectionism sets you up for high levels of stress and disappointment because it's impossible to be truly perfect.

Photoshop: a computer program that allows people to manipulate and change images, such as making a woman's legs appear longer and thinner.

Privacy Settings: allow you to change how much personal information other people can see on your online profiles. Privacy settings keep you safe from strangers and minimize opportunities for cyberbullying.

Projecting: assuming that someone else has the same thoughts or motivations as you. For example, if you cheated on a test and feel guilty, you might project the experience on someone else and accuse them of cheating, too.

Puberty: the period of life when your body transitions from being a kid's body to an adult's body, and the whole process is caused by the release of new hormones by your brain. Puberty usually starts between ages eight and thirteen in girls, although it's normal for girls to start earlier or later.

Real Food: Real Food is food that grows in nature or only has to be minimally processed before being eaten—like apples, green beans, whole wheat bread, meat, beans, or milk.

Registered Dietitian: a healthcare professional who teaches patients about proper food and nutrition in order to promote good health.

Relationship Aggression: an indirect form of bullying that is meant to cause damage to someone's relationships and social standing with others. Examples of relational aggression include telling secrets, spreading rumors, excluding, name-calling, lying, or cyberbullying.

Self-Compassion: going "easy" on yourself when you come across things you don't like about yourself or don't reach a goal.

Social Norm: something that people expect you to do in certain situations. Shaking hands when you meet a new person is a social norm; unfortunately, Fat Talking and bullying can also be social norms.

Stress: anything that causes you to feel extra bad or extra good, like your parents getting a divorce or landing the star role in the school play. You can reduce the physical and mental impact of stress by taking care of your body, thinking positive thoughts, and asking for help when you need it.

Teen-Esteem: the special kind of self-esteem that only kids and teens possess. When your teen-esteem is high, you have the confidence to try new things, make healthy choices, and stand up for yourself and others.

Thin Ideal: the idea of beauty for girls and women that the media has created over time through pictures in magazines and commercials on television. The Thin Ideal often says that women should all be skinny with straight teeth and silky hair. Images of the Thin Ideal are often Photoshopped—or fake—and can have a negative impact on our sense of self-esteem.

TOFI: stands for Thin on the Outside, Fat on the Inside. People who are TOFIs appear to be a healthy weight but have excess levels of body fat around their important internal organs. You can't see this extra fat, but it can cause many of the same health issues as being overweight.

Toxic Relationships: an interaction between two people that is harmful, emotionally or physically.

Inspiring Quotes

Life begins right outside your comfort zone. Try something NEW today!

Everyone starts somewhere. It's not where you start; it's where you end up that matters.

Attitudes are contagious. Is yours worth catching?

You don't have to be flawless to be beautiful. Beautiful is YOU!

Makeup is an accessory, not a necessity for beauty.

The best accessory is a confident smile!

Every breath is a second chance.

Scales measure weight, not worth.

Don't let your life be ruled by fear. Make choices that will get you closer to your goals!

Perhaps the most basic decision we must confront is whether to believe in ourselves and our own abilities.

Why would you want to be a copy of everyone else when you could be an original you?

Accept no one else's definition of your life. Define how you want to live.

You are the creator of your own future—do you want it to be positive or negative?

Don't fight who you are—celebrate it!

In the end, only kindness matters.

Words are powerful. They can heal you or hurt you. Speak to yourself kindly!

True beauty is in our hearts, not on our skin.

Just because you're different doesn't mean you're wrong. Different is beautiful!

Your beautiful body is perfect the way it is right now!

It takes courage to try something different or new.

Asking for help is a sign of strength.

You can choose to react to hurtful words with indifference. Walk away and keep your head held high!

Change the world—it starts with you.

The problem with fitting in is that you have to lose a bit of your special uniqueness to be just like everyone else.

Respect your body; it's the only one you have.

Thoughts become actions; think positively!

Happiness depends on you.

Take a diet from negative thoughts and fill yourself up with positive ones.

Health isn't a number on the scale. It's about how well you treat yourself, mentally and physically!

There could never be a more beautiful you!

Sources

Page 7: **Positive thinking:** www.mayoclinic.com/health/positive-thinking/SR00009

Page 26: **Recharge:** www.pets.webmd.com/slideshow-pets-improve-your-health

Page 27: **Afraid of being fat:** www.bodyimageprogram.org/action/ftfw/; **Bullied every seven minutes:** www.confidencecoalition.org/confidencecoaltionfacts_1; **Number one wish:** www.healthyplace.com/eating-disorders/main/eating-disorders-body-image-andadvertising/menu-id-58/; **Women earn less:** www.confidencecoalition.org/confidencecoaltionfacts_1; **Boys in the classroom:** D'Ambrosio, M, and P. S. Hammer. "Gender Equity in the Catholic Elementary Schools." Presented at the Annual Convention and Exposition of the National Catholic Education Association, Philadelphia, PA, April 1996.

Page 27: **More afraid of becoming fat:** www.colorado.edu/studentgroups/wellness/NewSite/BdyImgShockingStats.html

Page 46: **Be real:** www.sciencedaily.com/releases/2009/07/090702110503.htm

Page 54: **Relational aggression:** www.time.com/time/health/article/0,8599,2013184,00.html#ixzz17Stfo35J

Page 66: **Cyberspace:** opheliaproject.org/main/pdf/OPINFOPACKET%20oct08FINAL.pdf

Page 74: **Advertisements:** www.med.umich.edu/yourchild/topics/tv.htm; Harris Interactive Poll, 2007

Page 79: **Magazine sleuthing:** Nancy Signorelli, "A Content Analysis: Reflections of Girls in the Media," The Henry J. Kaiser Family Foundation and Children Now, April 1997.

Page 81: **Overestimate size:** www.healthyplace.com/eating-disorders/main/eating-disorders-body-imageand-advertising/menu-id-58/

Page 117: **Good for you:** Thoits P, and Lyndi Hewitt. "Volunteer work and well-being." *Journal of Health & Social Behavior* 42 no. 2 (June 2001):115–131.

Page 127: **Eat to become smarter:** www.livescience.com/health/080709-food-brain.html

Page 134: **Overweight kids:** www.kidshealth.org/kid/stay_healthy/body/overweight.html#cat118; **Get moving:** www.msnbc.msn.com/id/18594089/ns/health-fitness

Page 143: **Puberty:** kidshealth.org/teen/sexual_health/changing_body/puberty.html

Page 144: **Calories:** www.teengrowth.com/index.cfm?action=info_advice&ID_Advice=2434; www.tweenparenting.about.com/od/healthfitness/f/TweenCalories.htm

Page 145: **Diets don't work:** www.mann.bol.ucla.edu/files/Diets_don't_work.pdf

Page 156: **Breakfast and happy weight:** www.nutrition.about.com/od/nutrition101/a/breakfast.htm

Page 158: **Need more fuel:** www.circ.ahajournals.org/cgi/content/full/112/13/2061/TBL3

Page 160: **Changing taste buds:** www.kidshealth.org/kid/talk/qa/taste_buds.html

Page 162: **Water, water, everywhere:** www.kidshealth.org/teen/safety/first_aid/dehydration.html#

Page 172: **Screen time overload:** www.med.umich.edu/yourchild/topics/tv.htm; www.nytimes.com/2010/01/20/education/20wired.html

Page 178: **Exercise for an hour:** www.seventeen.com/health/tips/fhqa-081007

Acknowledgments

Operation Beautiful would have never spread without the dedication of thousands of loyal operationbeautiful.com and healthytippingpoint.com readers. I owe a huge thanks to every girl, woman, boy, and man who has ever participated in Operation Beautiful. This book is as much your book as it is mine. Thank you for spreading the love, from the very bottom of my heart.

A big thank-you goes out to the healthy living blog community—including other bloggers and our amazing readers. Your love of Operation Beautiful and willingness to promote the cause across the Internet was a huge factor in getting the mission to go viral. A great deal of debt is owed to each of you. Thank you, thank you. In particular, thanks to Anne P., who wrote about her experiences with bullying and Operation Beautiful on her lovely blog fANNEtasticfood.com and agreed to share the tale in this book. And big thanks to Heather Pare of hangrypants.com for sharing the wonderfully descriptive phrase "flower cutter" with me.

I owe Janel Ovrut a debt of gratitude as well. Janel is a registered dietitian and blogger behind eatwellwithjanel.com. Thank you, Janel, for proofreading the healthy eating chapter of this book and providing the expert insight into tween and teen eating.

Thanks to Molly Barker and the amazing staff at Girls on the Run (girlsontherun.org). Volunteering with this organization changed the way I saw the world, tween girls, and even myself. Girls on the Run has been an incredible blessing, and my experiences with this organization were instrumental in writing this book. Thank you for inspiring me.

Thanks to my awesome agent, Chris Park, who believed in Operation Beautiful and me from the start. Chris, you literally changed my entire life with a single e-mail. I'll never forget all you did for me. And a huge thanks to Laura Marchesani and the team at Grosset & Dunlap for recognizing a need for a girl-focused Operation Beautiful book. Laura, you've been a great editor, and I appreciate your wisdom so much.

Last, but not least, thank you to Kristien, Mom, Dad, Maggie and James, Sarah, Lauren, and the rest of my amazing friends. My life is so much richer because of you. Thank you for believing in me and supporting me. It means more to me than you can possibly ever know.